Volcanoes & Earthquakes

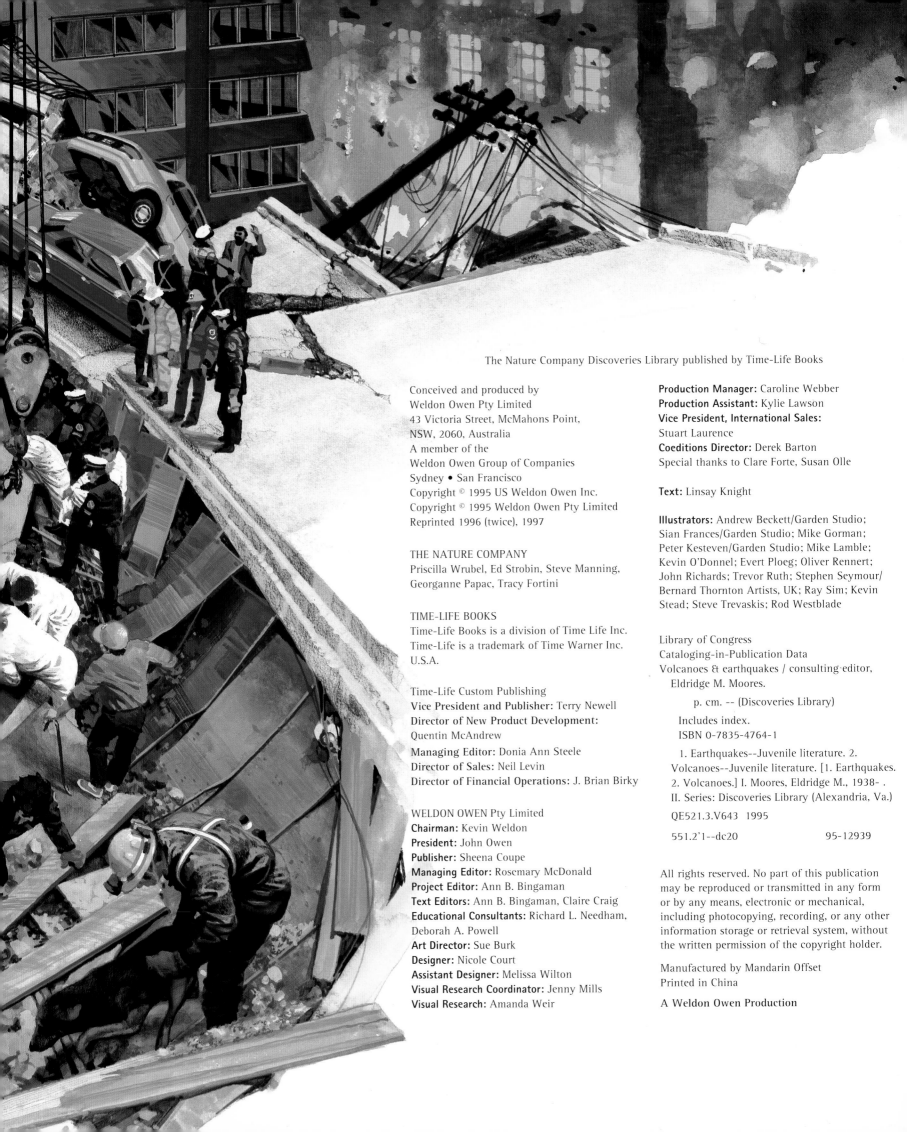

The Nature Company Discoveries Library published by Time-Life Books

Conceived and produced by
Weldon Owen Pty Limited
43 Victoria Street, McMahons Point,
NSW, 2060, Australia
A member of the
Weldon Owen Group of Companies
Sydney • San Francisco
Copyright © 1995 US Weldon Owen Inc.
Copyright © 1995 Weldon Owen Pty Limited
Reprinted 1996 (twice), 1997

THE NATURE COMPANY
Priscilla Wrubel, Ed Strobin, Steve Manning,
Georganne Papac, Tracy Fortini

TIME-LIFE BOOKS
Time-Life Books is a division of Time Life Inc.
Time-Life is a trademark of Time Warner Inc.
U.S.A.

Time-Life Custom Publishing
Vice President and Publisher: Terry Newell
Director of New Product Development:
Quentin McAndrew
Managing Editor: Donia Ann Steele
Director of Sales: Neil Levin
Director of Financial Operations: J. Brian Birky

WELDON OWEN Pty Limited
Chairman: Kevin Weldon
President: John Owen
Publisher: Sheena Coupe
Managing Editor: Rosemary McDonald
Project Editor: Ann B. Bingaman
Text Editors: Ann B. Bingaman, Claire Craig
Educational Consultants: Richard L. Needham,
Deborah A. Powell
Art Director: Sue Burk
Designer: Nicole Court
Assistant Designer: Melissa Wilton
Visual Research Coordinator: Jenny Mills
Visual Research: Amanda Weir

Production Manager: Caroline Webber
Production Assistant: Kylie Lawson
Vice President, International Sales:
Stuart Laurence
Coeditions Director: Derek Barton
Special thanks to Clare Forte, Susan Olle

Text: Linsay Knight

Illustrators: Andrew Beckett/Garden Studio;
Sian Frances/Garden Studio; Mike Gorman;
Peter Kesteven/Garden Studio; Mike Lamble;
Kevin O'Donnel; Evert Ploeg; Oliver Rennert;
John Richards; Trevor Ruth; Stephen Seymour/
Bernard Thornton Artists, UK; Ray Sim; Kevin
Stead; Steve Trevaskis; Rod Westblade

Library of Congress
Cataloging-in-Publication Data
Volcanoes & earthquakes / consulting editor,
    Eldridge M. Moores.
        p. cm. -- (Discoveries Library)
    Includes index.
    ISBN 0-7835-4764-1
    1. Earthquakes--Juvenile literature. 2.
Volcanoes--Juvenile literature. [1. Earthquakes.
2. Volcanoes.] I. Moores, Eldridge M., 1938- .
II. Series: Discoveries Library (Alexandria, Va.)
QE521.3.V643 1995
551.2'1--dc20   95-12939

Manufactured by Mandarin Offset
Printed in China

A Weldon Owen Production

THE NATURE COMPANY
DISCOVERIES
LIBRARY

Volcanoes &
Earthquakes

CONSULTING EDITOR

Dr. Eldridge M. Moores

Professor of Geology
University of California at Davis, California

TIME
LIFE
BOOKS

Contents

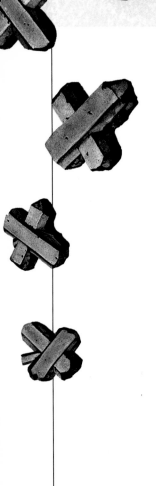

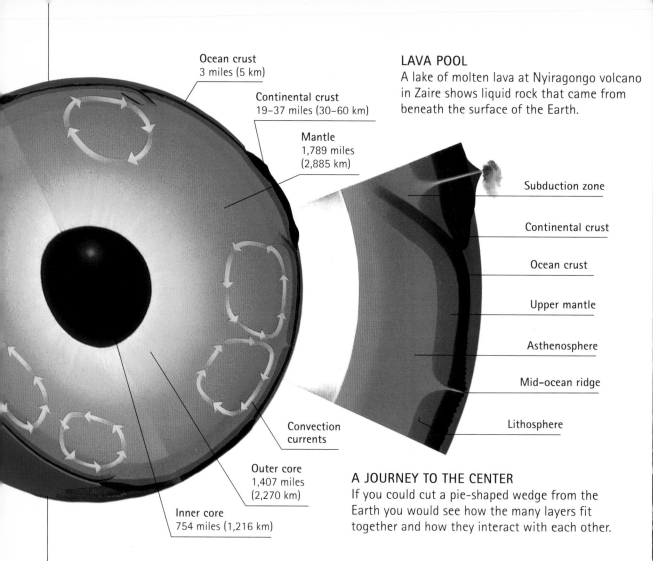

Ocean crust
3 miles (5 km)

Continental crust
19–37 miles (30–60 km)

Mantle
1,789 miles
(2,885 km)

LAVA POOL
A lake of molten lava at Nyiragongo volcano in Zaire shows liquid rock that came from beneath the surface of the Earth.

Subduction zone

Continental crust

Ocean crust

Upper mantle

Asthenosphere

Mid-ocean ridge

Lithosphere

Convection
currents

Outer core
1,407 miles
(2,270 km)

Inner core
754 miles (1,216 km)

A JOURNEY TO THE CENTER
If you could cut a pie-shaped wedge from the Earth you would see how the many layers fit together and how they interact with each other.

• THE UNSTABLE EARTH •

Fire Down Below

The Earth is made up of several layers. If you could stand at the center, 3,950 miles (6,371 km) down, you would see the solid iron inner core, which is surrounded by an outer core of liquid iron and nickel. To travel to the surface, you would pass through the solid rock of the lower mantle, then the soft, squishy area of rock called the asthenosphere. The final two layers join together to form the lithosphere, which is made up of the solid rock of the upper mantle, and the crust. The crust covers the Earth as thin apple peel covers an apple. Inside the Earth, radioactive elements decay and produce heat, and the temperature increases to an amazing 5,432°F (3,000°C) at the core. This heat provides the energy for the layers to move and interact. Melted rock called magma rises from deep within the Earth to near the surface. Some of it cools and becomes solid within the crust but some erupts on the surface as lava.

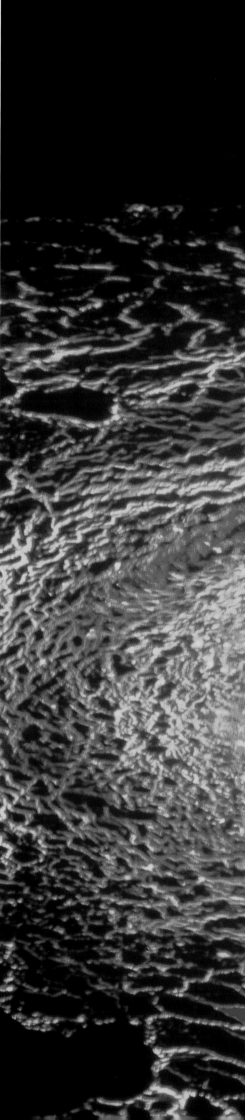

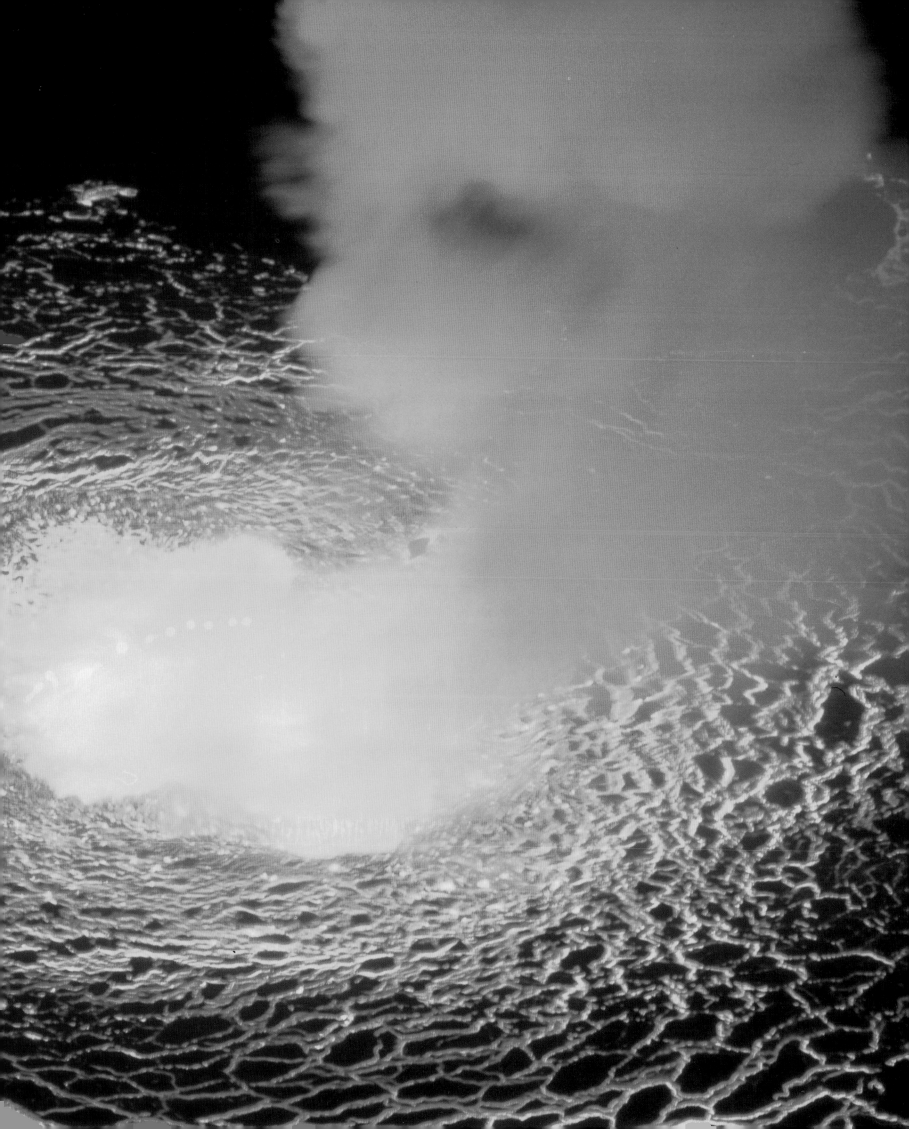

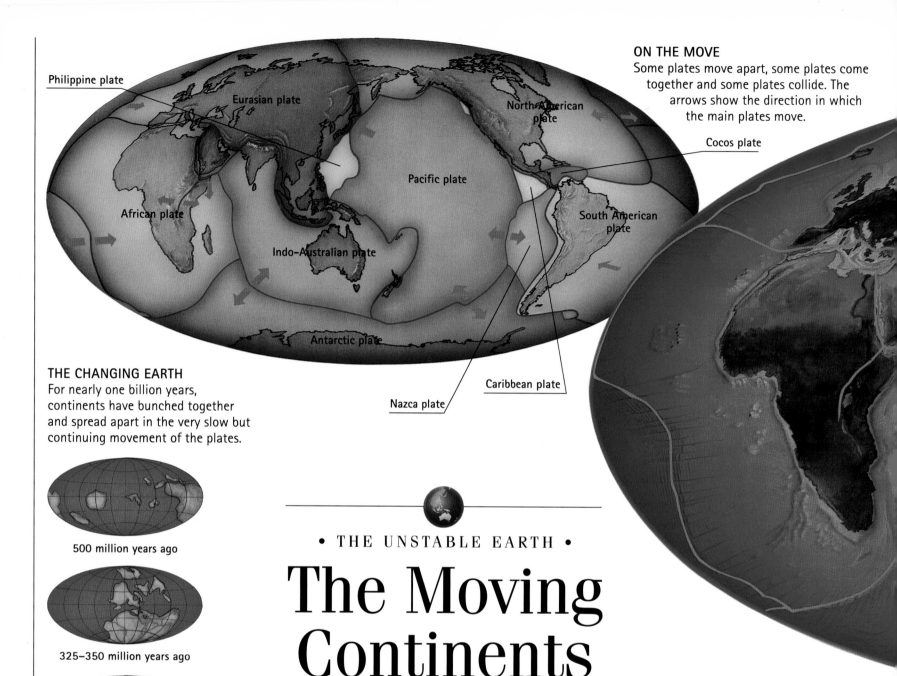

Philippine plate
Eurasian plate
North American plate
Pacific plate
African plate
Indo-Australian plate
South American plate
Antarctic plate
Cocos plate
Caribbean plate
Nazca plate

ON THE MOVE
Some plates move apart, some plates come together and some plates collide. The arrows show the direction in which the main plates move.

THE CHANGING EARTH
For nearly one billion years, continents have bunched together and spread apart in the very slow but continuing movement of the plates.

500 million years ago

325–350 million years ago

Pangaea the supercontinent
200 million years ago

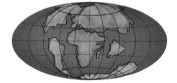

Pangaea splits into
Gondwana and Laurasia
130 million years ago

Gondwana and Laurasia
65 million years ago

• THE UNSTABLE EARTH •

The Moving Continents

The Earth's outermost section, the lithosphere, is separated into seven large and several small jagged slabs called lithospheric plates, which fit together much like puzzle pieces. The crust, or top part, of each two-layered plate comes from either an ocean, a continent or a bit of both. You cannot feel it, but the plates are constantly moving. Supported by the soft, squishy material of the asthenosphere under them, plates pull and push against each other at a rate of 3/4–8 in (2–20 cm) per year. When plates pull apart, magma from the mantle erupts and forms new ocean crust. When they move together, one plate slowly dives under the other and forms a deep ocean trench. Mountain ranges form when some plates collide. Other plates slide and scrape past each other. Most volcanoes and earthquakes occur along edges where plates meet.

A NEW THEORY
In 1915, Alfred Wegener, a German scientist and explorer, proposed his theory of continental drift. He wrote of a huge supercontinent, Pangaea, which split apart millions of years ago. The pieces then slowly drifted to their present position. Not until the mid-1960s was the theory revised and accepted by scientists.

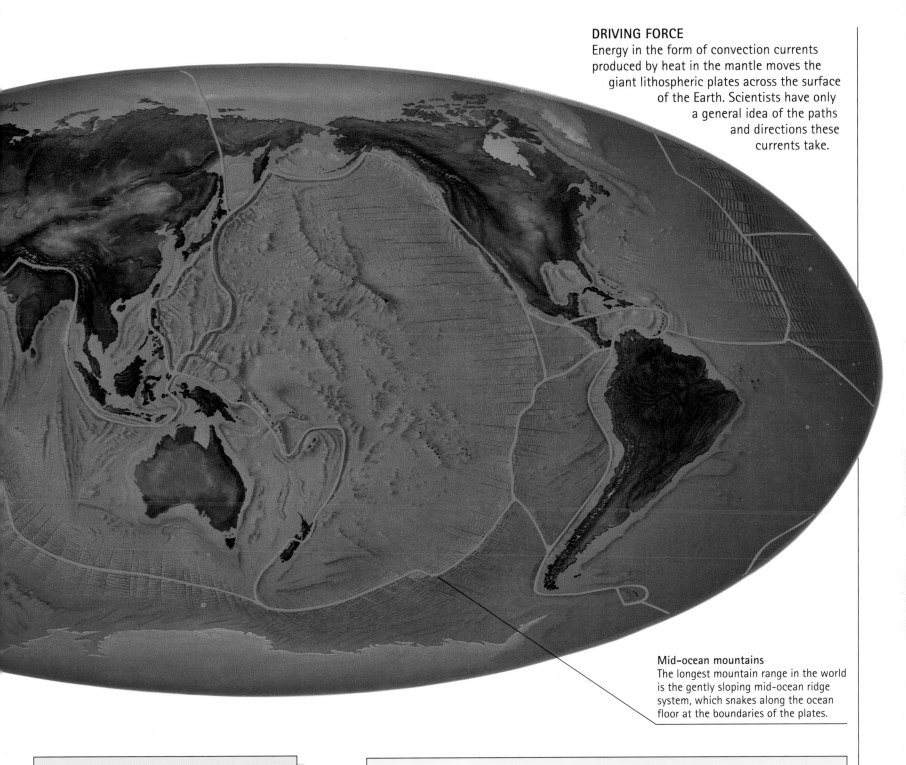

DRIVING FORCE

Energy in the form of convection currents produced by heat in the mantle moves the giant lithospheric plates across the surface of the Earth. Scientists have only a general idea of the paths and directions these currents take.

Mid-ocean mountains
The longest mountain range in the world is the gently sloping mid-ocean ridge system, which snakes along the ocean floor at the boundaries of the plates.

STRANGE BUT TRUE

Many millions of years ago, the east coast of South America and the west coast of Africa fitted together as part of the same land mass. Today, the two continents even have similar rock, plant and animal fossils.

Glossopteris

SLIDING BY

When some plates meet they slide past each other in opposite directions or in the same direction at different speeds. The edges of the sliding plates grind when they meet, causing a series of weblike cracks or faults and fractures to occur. Here an orchard changes course to follow the line of a fault—a simple example of plate movement. As the two plates move slowly past each other, stress builds up in the rocks below and an earthquake can occur.

Discover more in Fire Down Below

Ridges and Rift Valleys

The ocean crust is rugged with mountain ridges and deep rift valleys or cracks. When two plates with ocean crust move apart, magma from the mantle bubbles up to the surface to fill the rift. The magma cools and hardens and adds new strips of crust or ocean floor to the edges of the two plates. This forms what is called a spreading, or widening, ridge. The Atlantic Ocean is widening by ³/₄ in (2 cm) per year. The East Pacific Rise is widening by 8 in (20 cm) per year—the fastest widening rate of an ocean floor. In 10 million years, it will be 1,240 miles (2,000 km) wider. Plates continue to move away from the spreading ridge towards other plates. When a spreading ridge fractures or breaks, earthquakes occur. Mid-ocean ridge volcanoes also form in rifts, fed by the magma from below. Over millions of years, they can grow so large that they rise above the water to form islands, such as Iceland on the North Atlantic mid-ocean ridge.

Smoking chimneys
Sulfur and other minerals deposited on the sides of the vents build natural chimneys of up to 33 feet (10 m) high.

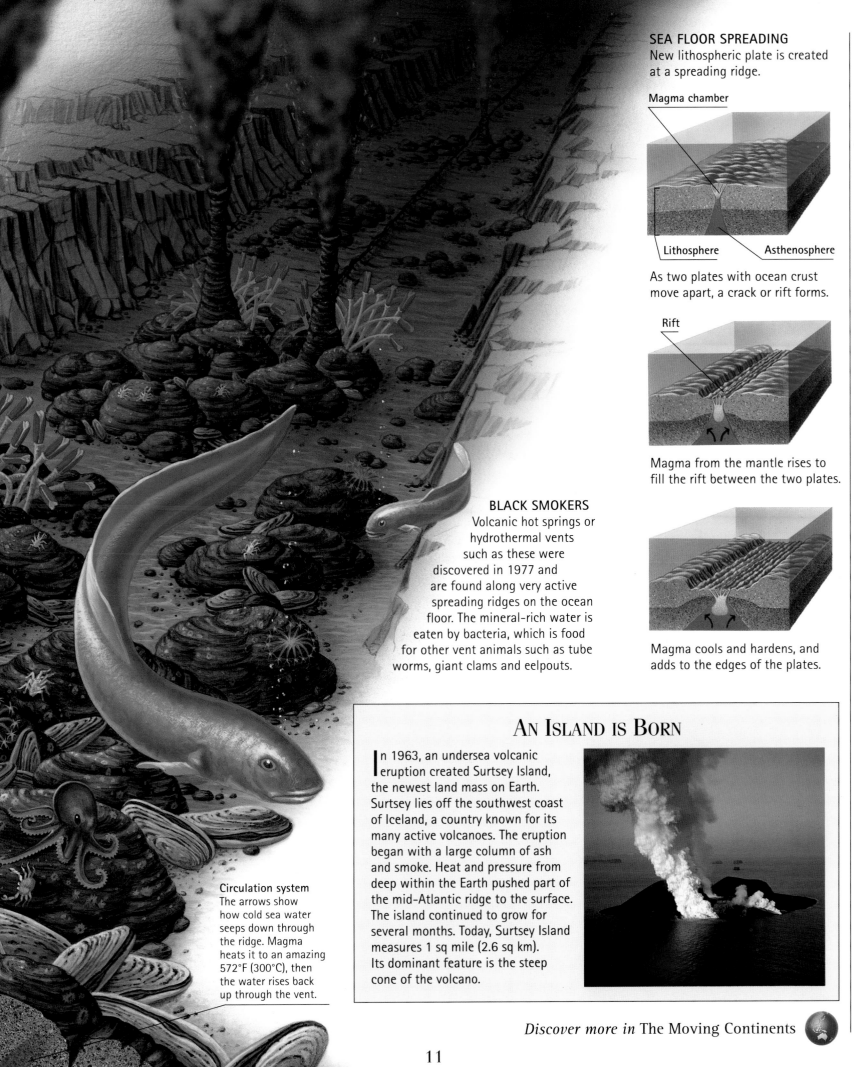

SEA FLOOR SPREADING
New lithospheric plate is created at a spreading ridge.

Magma chamber

Lithosphere   Asthenosphere

As two plates with ocean crust move apart, a crack or rift forms.

Rift

Magma from the mantle rises to fill the rift between the two plates.

Magma cools and hardens, and adds to the edges of the plates.

BLACK SMOKERS
Volcanic hot springs or hydrothermal vents such as these were discovered in 1977 and are found along very active spreading ridges on the ocean floor. The mineral-rich water is eaten by bacteria, which is food for other vent animals such as tube worms, giant clams and eelpouts.

AN ISLAND IS BORN

In 1963, an undersea volcanic eruption created Surtsey Island, the newest land mass on Earth. Surtsey lies off the southwest coast of Iceland, a country known for its many active volcanoes. The eruption began with a large column of ash and smoke. Heat and pressure from deep within the Earth pushed part of the mid-Atlantic ridge to the surface. The island continued to grow for several months. Today, Surtsey Island measures 1 sq mile (2.6 sq km). Its dominant feature is the steep cone of the volcano.

Circulation system
The arrows show how cold sea water seeps down through the ridge. Magma heats it to an amazing 572°F (300°C), then the water rises back up through the vent.

Discover more in The Moving Continents

11

Subduction

When two plates move toward each other and meet, one plate slowly dives, or subducts, beneath the other along what is called a "subduction zone." This is an area of intense earthquake and volcanic activity caused by the movement of the two plates. There are three types of plate boundaries where subduction occurs: ocean to ocean, ocean to continent and continent to continent. The action of subduction is the same for all three types but the results are different. The area at which one plate dives beneath another creates an ocean trench, the deepest part of the ocean floor. As the down-going plate continues to sink deeper into the mantle, it mixes with hot rock and melts to form magma. Under extreme heat and pressure, this new magma mixture then forces its way back upwards to erupt violently at the surface. Compared to the gentle chain of mid-ocean ridge volcanoes, subduction volcanoes are explosive and dangerous. This is due to the presence of water and the build-up of gases dissolved in the thick and sticky magma that is produced in the process of subduction.

OCEAN TO OCEAN
When two plates with ocean crust meet, one plate subducts. When the magma rises to the surface, it forms an island arc volcano chain such as the Lesser Antilles in the East Caribbean.

Island arc volcano

Ocean crust

Magma

Subduction zone

Asthenosphere

OCEAN TO CONTINENT
When a plate with thin ocean crust meets a plate with thicker continental crust, the thinner plate subducts. Magma rises to the surface and forms a line of volcanoes such as these on the west coast of South America.

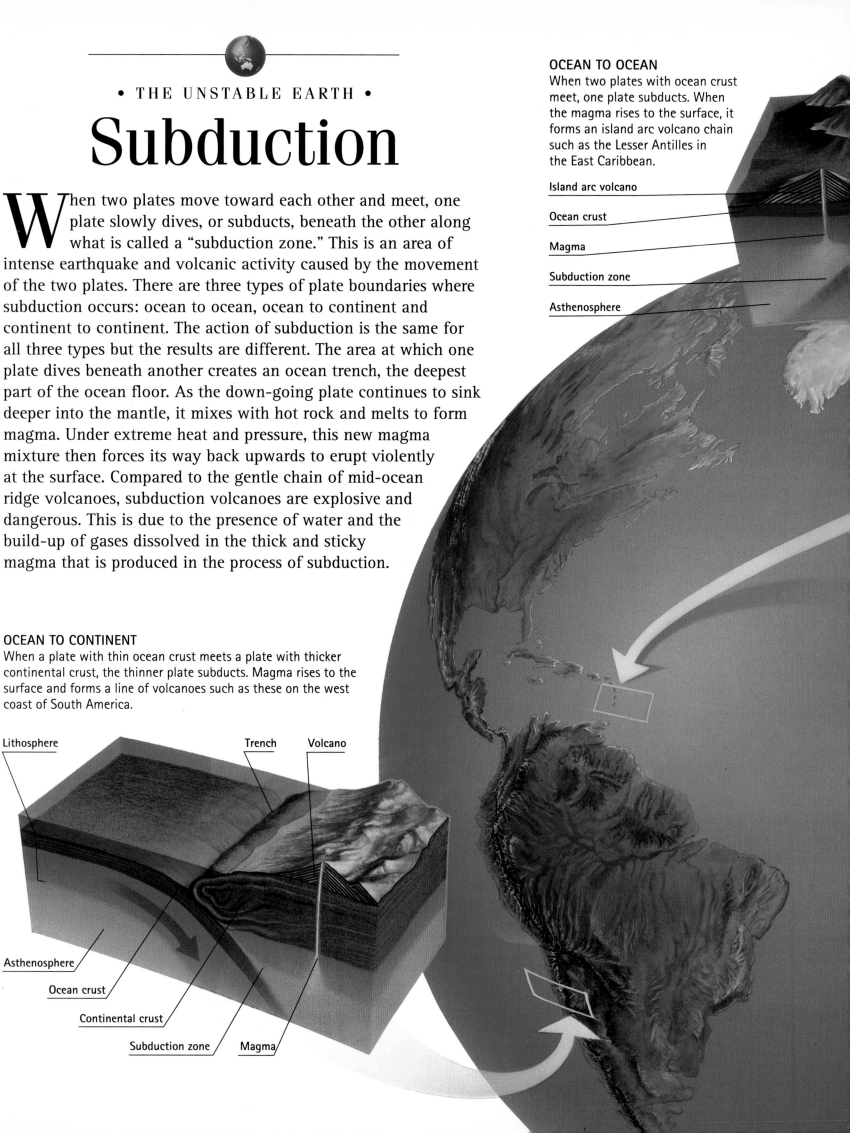

Lithosphere

Trench

Volcano

Asthenosphere

Ocean crust

Continental crust

Subduction zone

Magma

Trench   Ocean crust   Lithosphere

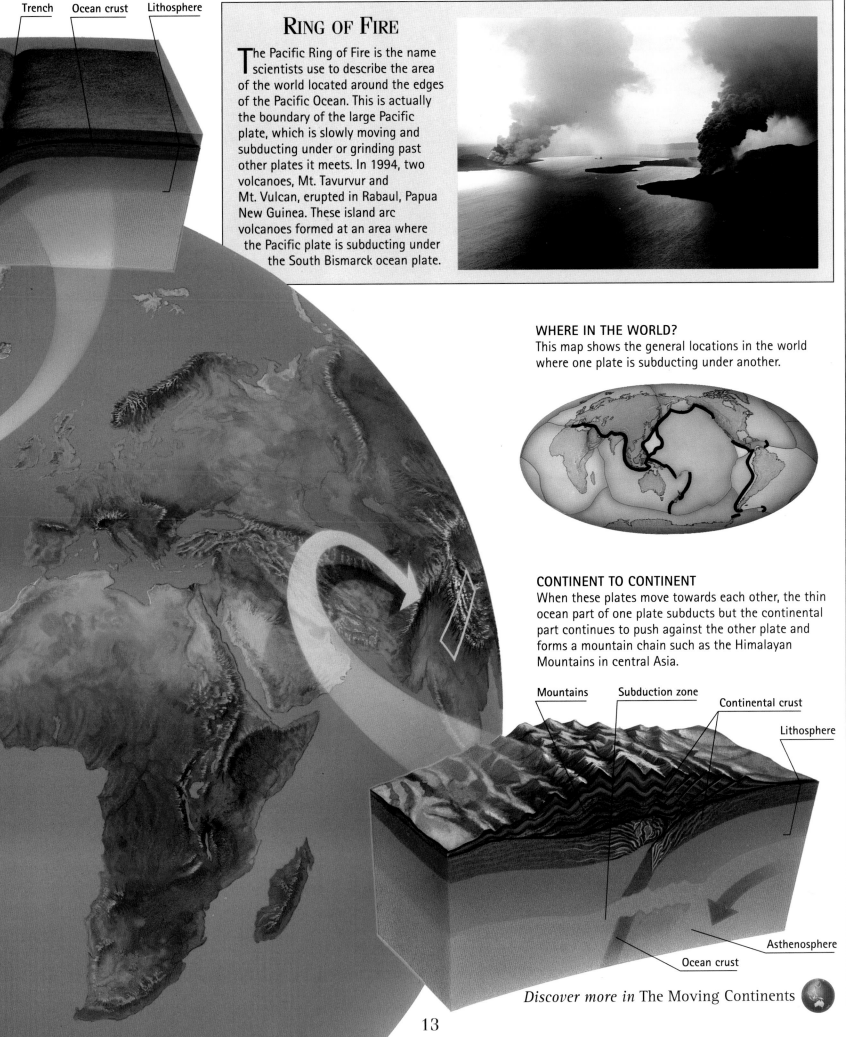

RING OF FIRE

The Pacific Ring of Fire is the name scientists use to describe the area of the world located around the edges of the Pacific Ocean. This is actually the boundary of the large Pacific plate, which is slowly moving and subducting under or grinding past other plates it meets. In 1994, two volcanoes, Mt. Tavurvur and Mt. Vulcan, erupted in Rabaul, Papua New Guinea. These island arc volcanoes formed at an area where the Pacific plate is subducting under the South Bismarck ocean plate.

WHERE IN THE WORLD?
This map shows the general locations in the world where one plate is subducting under another.

CONTINENT TO CONTINENT
When these plates move towards each other, the thin ocean part of one plate subducts but the continental part continues to push against the other plate and forms a mountain chain such as the Himalayan Mountains in central Asia.

Mountains   Subduction zone   Continental crust   Lithosphere

Asthenosphere   Ocean crust

Discover more in The Moving Continents

13

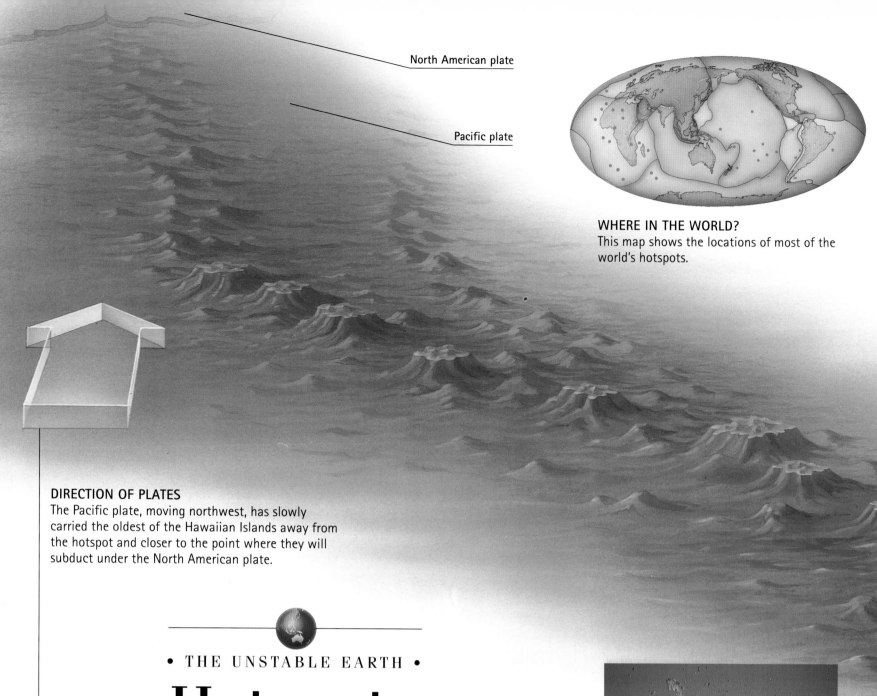

North American plate

Pacific plate

WHERE IN THE WORLD?
This map shows the locations of most of the world's hotspots.

DIRECTION OF PLATES
The Pacific plate, moving northwest, has slowly carried the oldest of the Hawaiian Islands away from the hotspot and closer to the point where they will subduct under the North American plate.

• THE UNSTABLE EARTH •

Hotspots

Volcanoes are born in different ways and hotspot volcanoes, though spectacular, are often less violent than those that occur at subduction zones. Hotspot volcanoes form in the middle of plates, directly above a source of magma. Molten rock rises to the surface from deep within the Earth's mantle, pierces the plate like a blow torch and erupts in a lava flow or fountain. A hotspot stays still, but the plate keeps moving. Over millions of years this process forms a string of volcanic islands such as the Hawaiian Island chain on the Pacific plate. Hawaii's Mauna Loa and Kilauea, now active volcanoes, will gradually become dormant or cold as Hawaii moves off the hotspot. A new active volcano, such as Loihi to the southeast, might become a new island above the hotspot. The Pacific plate has carried other island volcanoes in the chain far away from the magma source.

INDIAN OCEAN VOLCANO
Piton de la Fournaise on Réunion Island is one of the most active volcanoes in the world.

KILAUEA FLOWS
The lava that erupts from hotspot volcanoes such as Kilauea in Hawaii can move at speeds of up to 62 miles (100 km) per hour.

HOTSPOT, CONTINENTAL STYLE

Yellowstone National Park, in Wyoming, has spectacular geysers and natural hot springs and is one of the most famous hotspots found on a continent. Underground water is heated by a hotspot source of magma deep within the mantle. The steam in the boiling water expands, and water and steam burst through the many cracks in the crust and erupt as geysers. Some scientists believe that one day, in the next few hundred thousand years, a major volcanic eruption could occur in the area.

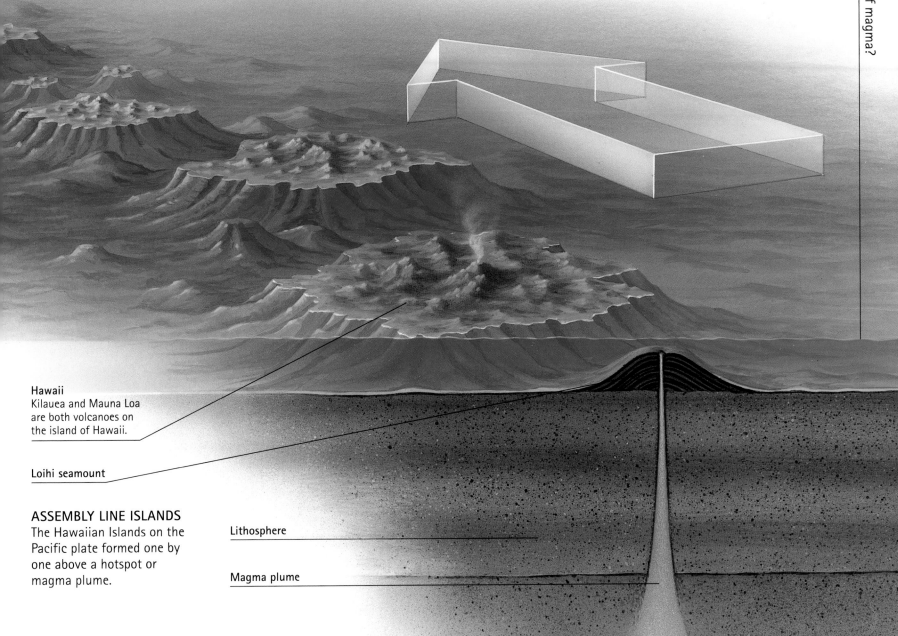

Hawaii
Kilauea and Mauna Loa are both volcanoes on the island of Hawaii.

Loihi seamount

ASSEMBLY LINE ISLANDS
The Hawaiian Islands on the Pacific plate formed one by one above a hotspot or magma plume.

Lithosphere

Magma plume

ACCORDING TO LEGEND
The ancient Greeks thought that Hephaistos, the god of fire, lived beneath Mt. Etna in Sicily where he made weapons for the gods. When he beat the red-hot iron, fire leapt out of the volcano above.

• THE UNSTABLE EARTH •

Myths and Legends

For thousands of years, different cultures have told similar tales of powerful forces and superhuman gods to explain volcanic eruptions or earthquakes. Many myths blame these events on the anger of the gods or evil demons that live in volcanoes and from time to time punish their human subjects. The ancient Greeks thought that a volcano destroyed the island of Atlantis because its people became too wealthy and proud. The ancient Romans believed that their god of fire, Vulcan, lived and stoked his blacksmith's furnace in a workshop beneath the present-day island of Vulcano. Hundreds of years ago, the Aztecs of Mexico and the people of Nicaragua believed gods lived in the lava lakes. They sacrificed beautiful young girls to these powerful gods.

STRANGE BUT TRUE

In 1660, little black crosses rained down on the people of Naples—proof to many that St. Januarius was looking after them. The crosses were really twinned pyroxene crystals, which the Mt. Vesuvius volcano had hurled out of its crater.

PELÉ

Pelé, the Hawaiian goddess of fire and volcanoes, supposedly lives in the crater of Kilauea volcano on Hawaii. She is thought to be responsible for the many volcanic eruptions on the island. In ancient times Pelé was greatly feared as she destroyed villages with her lava. Today she is still very much a part of Hawaiian folklore. Pelé has a terrible temper and she throws lava at anyone who speaks out against her. Pelé is also angered by anyone who steals her lava. Some people have been known to send back lava samples they have taken from the Hawaii Volcanoes National Park because of the bad luck they associate with an angry Pelé. There are also stories of lava flows avoiding the homes of people who declared loudly their trust in her. Many people claim to have seen Pelé before a volcanic eruption when she appears as a wrinkled old woman or a beautiful young girl. Others say they see her image in the glow of an eruption.

A BALANCING ACT

According to an ancient Hindu myth, the Earth is carried on the back of an elephant, which stands on a turtle that is balanced on a cobra. Whenever one moves, the Earth trembles and shakes.

17

Volcanic Eruptions

HAWAIIAN
Large amounts of runny lava erupt and produce large, low volcanoes.

PELÉEAN
Blocks of thick, sticky lava are followed by a burning cloud of ash and gas.

STROMBOLIAN
Small, sticky lava bombs and blocks, ash, gas and glowing cinders erupt.

VULCANIAN
Violent explosions shoot out very thick lava and large lava bombs.

PLINIAN
Cinders, gas and ash erupt great distances into the air.

Deep inside the Earth, magma rises upwards, gathers in pools within or below the crust and tries to get to the surface. Cracks provide escape routes, and the magma erupts as a volcano. Steam and gas form clouds of white smoke, small fragments of rock and lava blow out as volcanic ash and cinder, and small hot bombs of lava shoot out and harden. Not all lava is the same. It may be thick and sticky or thin and runny. Lava thickness, or viscosity, determines the type of volcanic eruption and the kind of rock that forms when the lava hardens. Some volcanoes are active, erupting at any time; some are dormant or cold, waiting to erupt; others are dead or extinct. Volcanoes have shaped many of the Earth's islands, mountains and plains. They have also been responsible for changing weather, burying cities and killing people who live nearby.

THE INSIDE STORY
This cross-section shows the inner workings of a volcano and what happens during an eruption.

Side vent
Under pressure, this side vent branches off from the central vent and carries lava upwards through cracks in the rocks to ooze out the side of the volcano.

Why People Live Near Volcanoes

For centuries communities have grown up in the shadows of volcanoes. In Iceland, people use the energy from their island's many volcanoes to provide heat and power. Other people live near volcanoes because the soil is rich, and farmers grow crops and graze their herds on the slopes. In Indonesia more people live on the islands with active volcanoes than on the islands with none. Shown here are lush rice terraces growing on the fertile ground near the volcano Mt. Agung in Bali, Indonesia.

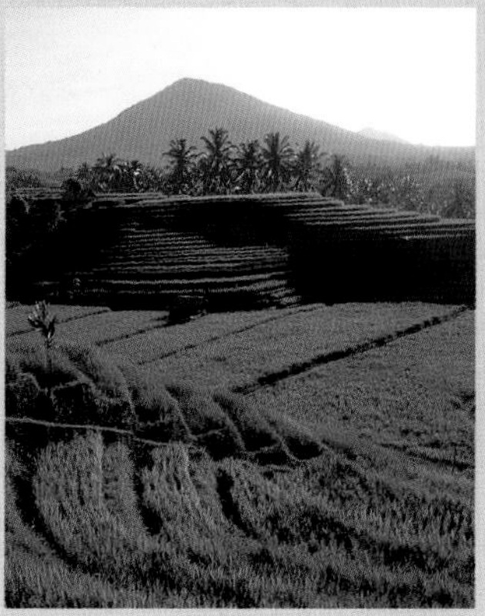

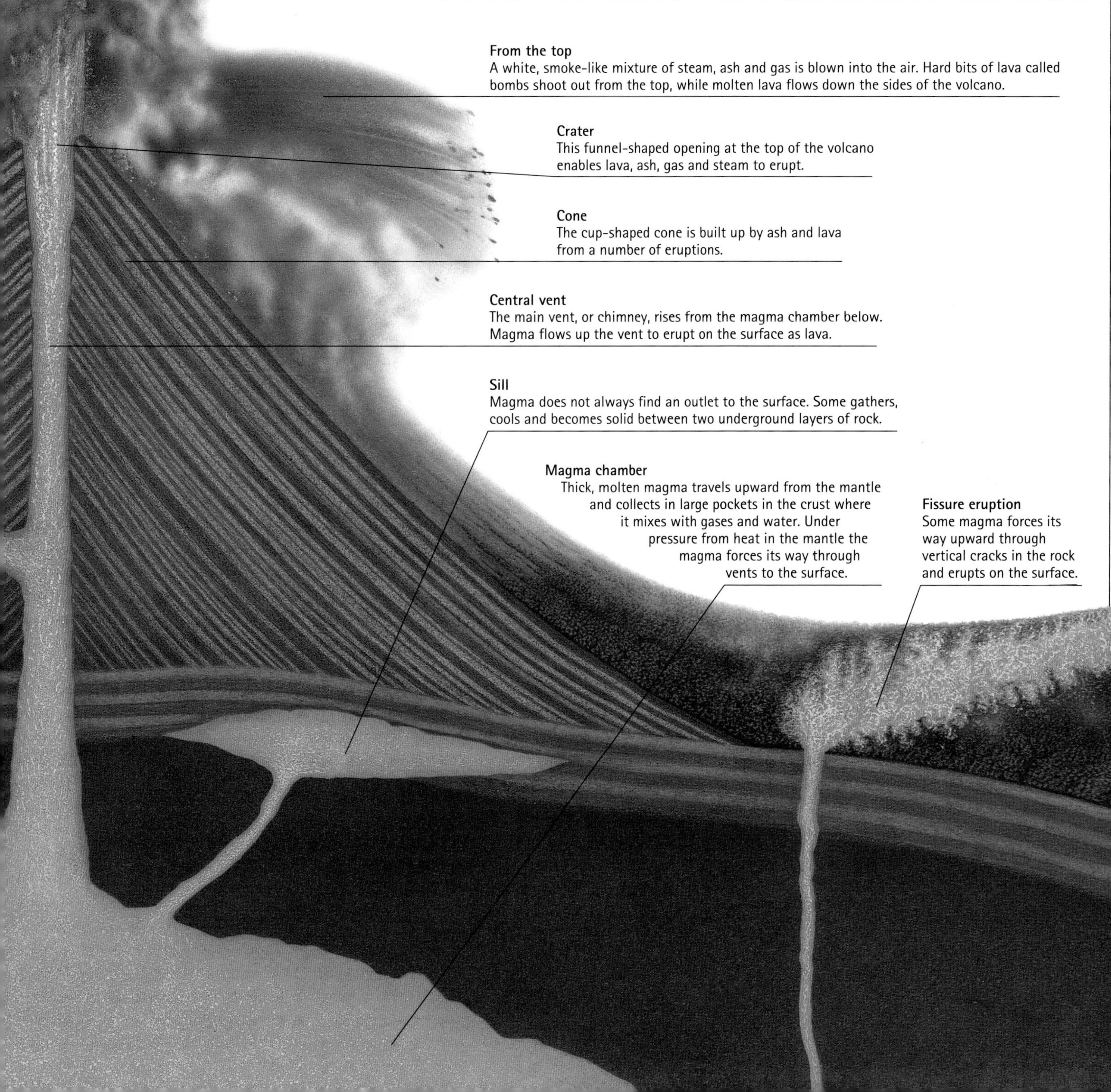

From the top
A white, smoke-like mixture of steam, ash and gas is blown into the air. Hard bits of lava called bombs shoot out from the top, while molten lava flows down the sides of the volcano.
Crater
This funnel-shaped opening at the top of the volcano enables lava, ash, gas and steam to erupt.
Cone
The cup-shaped cone is built up by ash and lava from a number of eruptions.
Central vent
The main vent, or chimney, rises from the magma chamber below. Magma flows up the vent to erupt on the surface as lava.
Sill
Magma does not always find an outlet to the surface. Some gathers, cools and becomes solid between two underground layers of rock.
Magma chamber
Thick, molten magma travels upward from the mantle and collects in large pockets in the crust where it mixes with gases and water. Under pressure from heat in the mantle the magma forces its way through vents to the surface.
Fissure eruption
Some magma forces its way upward through vertical cracks in the rock and erupts on the surface.

Q: What can happen to magma when it rises to the surface?

Lava Flows

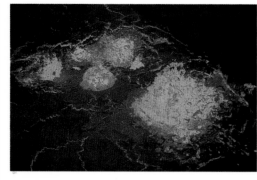

LAVA LAKES
Lava collects in a series of pools after the eruption of Pu'u O'o in Hawaii.

INTO THE SEA
Runny lava gushes from the side of a Hawaiian volcano into the sea below, where it cools.

Lava is red-hot magma that erupts at the Earth's surface. A river of runny lava flows downhill from a volcano's central crater or oozes from a crack in the ground. It cools down from temperatures of up to 2,192°F (1,200°C), becomes stickier and slower-moving and often forms volcanic rock called basalt. Explosive, killer subduction volcanoes erupt thick, sticky lava that contains large amounts of silica. This cools to form rocks such as rhyolite, and different forms of volcanic glass such as obsidian. Blocked outlets or large amounts of gas or water in the lava cause violent eruptions, with lava bombs and boulders shooting out in all directions. If lava hardens with a rough, broken surface, it is called "aa". Lava that hardens with a smoother covering skin is called "pahoehoe". Pahoehoe can wrinkle to form ropes of rock. Hardened lava often cracks to form regular columns.

TYPES OF LAVA FLOW

Lava is named according to how it looks as it cools and hardens. Pillow lava is the most common form of lava found on Earth. It erupts in water especially along the mid-ocean ridge where volcanoes gently ooze pillow-shaped lumps of lava through cracks in the ocean floor. Pillow lava can also be found on dry land that was once part of the ocean floor. Pahoehoe lava is runny and very fast-flowing. The surface cools quickly and forms a thin, smooth skin with hot lava still moving underneath, which can twist and coil the surface to look like rope. Aa lava flows move more slowly and are not as hot as pahoehoe. Aa flows cool to form sharp chunks of rock, which can be as thick as 328 feet (100 m).

Pillow lava

Pahoehoe lava

Aa lava

RIVER OF FIRE
In this Hawaiian-type eruption, the lava streams down from the volcano into an area where it burns houses and adds a new layer of volcanic rock to the ground.

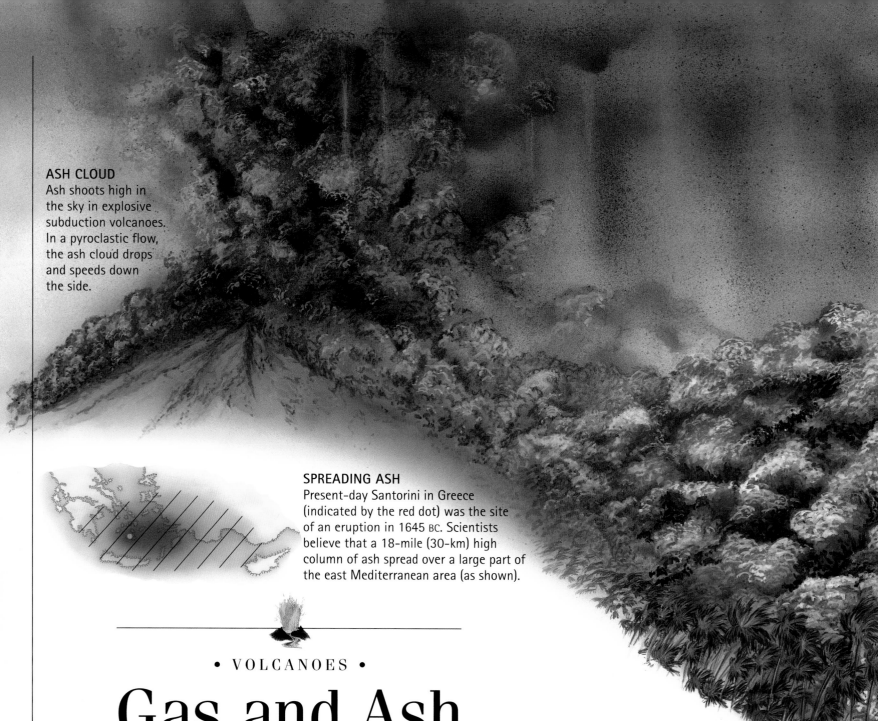

ASH CLOUD
Ash shoots high in the sky in explosive subduction volcanoes. In a pyroclastic flow, the ash cloud drops and speeds down the side.

SPREADING ASH
Present-day Santorini in Greece (indicated by the red dot) was the site of an eruption in 1645 BC. Scientists believe that a 18-mile (30-km) high column of ash spread over a large part of the east Mediterranean area (as shown).

• VOLCANOES •

Gas and Ash

As magma rises to the Earth's surface, the gases mixed in with it expand or swell and try to escape. These gases sometimes contain carbon dioxide and hydrogen sulphide, which are both very harmful to humans. In runny magma, gases have no trouble escaping and cause mild eruptions with a lava flow. Gases trapped in thick, sticky lava build up and explode violently. These explosive eruptions fling clouds of rock fragments and hardened lava froth called pumice several miles into the air. Ash is formed during the explosion when rock and lava blow apart into millions of tiny pieces. Falling ash spreads further and does more damage than lava flows do, although a small sprinkling of ash can add important nutrients to the soil. Sometimes the wind carries clouds of ash around the world, affecting weather patterns.

COVERED IN ASH
Residents in protective masks walk down a street in Olongapo City in the Philippines after the ash-fall from the 1991 eruption of Mt. Pinatubo.

22

MAURICE AND KATIA KRAFFT

French volcanologist Maurice Krafft and his geochemist wife Katia were responsible for some of the world's most spectacular volcano photographs. They witnessed more than 150 volcanic eruptions throughout the world and wrote many books and films. Their field work often placed them in great danger, and they had to wear heat-resistant suits for close-up photography. Both died in 1991 while they were filming a pyroclastic flow from the eruption of Mt. Unzen in Japan.

PYROCLASTIC ROCKS

Small fragments of volcanic rock and frothy pumice fly into the air. Larger bombs or blocks, some the size of boulders, bounce down the side of the mountain.

Q: What makes ash from a volcano dangerous?

PYROCLASTIC FLOW

This rapidly moving avalanche of volcanic fragments and gases, at a temperature of 212° F (100° C), can rocket down the side of a volcano at speeds of up to 155 miles (250 km) per hour, destroying everything in its path.

• VOLCANOES •

In the Field

Scientists who study volcanoes are called volcanologists. They observe the activity of a volcano so they can try to predict when an eruption might occur. Volcanologists often conduct field work near the craters or on the slopes of active volcanoes, where they collect samples of lava and gas and measure any temperature changes. They watch for an increase of ash and fumes erupting from the crater. Minor earthquake activity recorded on seismometers set up on a volcano's slopes can also warn volcanologists of a possible eruption. At Kilauea volcano in Hawaii there are observatories near the vent where scientists have spent years recording details of its day-to-day life. A study of this kind provides information about a particular type of volcano and helps scientists to forecast future activity. Not all eruptions are predictable, however, and some happen with no warning.

ROBOT VOLCANOLOGIST
This robotlike instrument called Dante
was designed to crawl inside the crater of
Mt. Erebus in Antarctica
to monitor gas and lava.

DID YOU KNOW?
Volcanologists use a special electric
thermometer called a thermocouple
to take a volcano's temperature.
Lava is so hot that a glass
thermometer would melt.

VOLCANO WORKSHOP

In 1988, after nearly 40 years of silence, Galeras volcano in Colombia showed signs of activity. An international workshop for scientists was set up there in 1993 to research and monitor the volcano. These scientists did their field work on the slopes and in the crater of Galeras. On 14 January one group was working in the crater taking measurements and samples of gases. As the group left the crater the volcano erupted, killing nine people and injuring five more. The explosion caused a 2-mile (3-km) high plume of ash and gas. The scientists had been careful but the volcano did the unexpected.

Subduction zone volcano
Galeras is 14,006-ft (4,270-m) high. The crater is 4 miles (6 km) from Pasto, a city with more than 300,000 people.

Collecting data
Scientists take gas samples from the edge of the inner crater where three men died when Galeras exploded 16 days earlier.

WORLDWIDE EFFECT

A powerful volcano can shoot huge amounts of ash, gas and dust upwards through the troposphere and into the stratosphere where strong winds carry it to all parts of the globe.

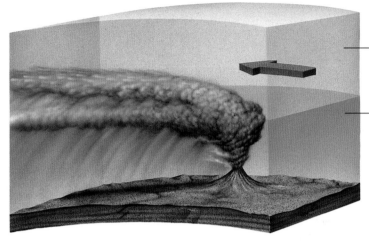

Stratosphere

Troposphere

• AFTER THE EVENT •

Under the Weather

Volcanic eruptions produce a variety of hazards and changes to the environment. After an eruption, the local area may experience months of strong winds, heavy rain and mudflows. Clouds of fine volcanic ash blown into the air affect people's breathing. The engines of aircraft flying in the area can become clogged with volcanic glass, dust and ash. Gas and ash ejected high enough into the stratosphere can travel all over the globe causing spectacular sunsets around the world. Weather patterns change in some areas, as clouds of sulphur-rich gases reflect the sun's rays back into space and the Earth below cools. This kills plants and crops and affects the animals that feed on this vegetation. In many parts of the world, volcanic twilights occur as sunlight is reduced and the temperature drops, producing long, cold winters.

FIREWORKS
Static electricity caused by colliding particles of ash and lava sparks bolts of lightning that crack in a fearsome display over an erupting volcano.

THE OZONE HOLE
This satellite picture shows the hole in the ozone layer. The hole gets bigger when damaging chemicals from volcanoes are erupted into the atmosphere.

NIGHT AT MIDDAY
The ash that fell from the 1982 eruption of Galunggung in Indonesia turned daylight skies to night.

THE YEAR WITHOUT A SUMMER

Dramatic changes in worldwide weather conditions followed the 1815 eruption of Tambora in Indonesia. Ash from the volcano shot into the stratosphere and was carried all around the world, which lowered temperatures in some countries. Summer frost and snow damaged food crops in parts of Europe and Scandinavia, causing widespread starvation. Unseasonable snowfalls also destroyed crops in the northeast section of the United States. The sky in this famous painting by British artist J.M.W. Turner shows the yellow haze caused by the volcanic dust that settled over Europe after the eruption.

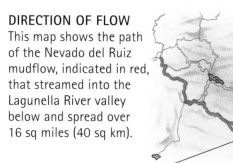

Nevado del Ruiz

Armero

MUDFLOW
In November 1985, the eruption of Nevado del Ruiz in Colombia melted ice and snow, which caused a devastating mudflow. Armero, 31 miles (50 km) away, was engulfed in a 131-ft (40-m) wall of mud and ash, which killed more than 23,000 people.

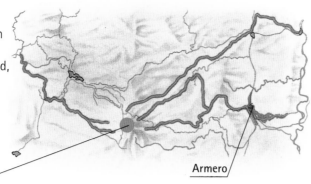

• AFTER THE EVENT •

Mudflows and Avalanches

Mudflows and avalanches can be triggered by volcanic eruptions and earthquakes. Explosive eruptions can leave volcanoes covered with a layer of ash, which becomes like thick, wet cement when mixed with water from melting ice or thunderstorms. The resulting mudflows, called "lahars," start to move downhill, gathering speed as they go. Stones, boulders, tree trunks and building rubble are picked up along the way. These moving streams of mud are often more powerful than rivers of water and can kill thousands of people and cause enormous damage over a widespread area before the mud sets as hard as concrete. In an avalanche, ash near a volcano's crater can collapse and carry away part of a mountain. Snow and rock may become airborne and travel at great speeds, crashing from a mountain top to a valley below in minutes.

MIRACLE RESCUE
Survivors were found up to three weeks after the eruption of Nevado del Ruiz. Relief workers from many parts of the world arrived with emergency supplies to help the survivors. Here, workers wash the mud off a rescued child.

LUCKY SURVIVOR
Fewer than 3,000 people survived the mudflow from Nevado del Ruiz, which destroyed the town of Armero.

AVALANCHE!
An earthquake off the coast of Peru in 1960 triggered an avalanche from Huascaran mountain. Snow and rock fell 13,120 ft (4,000 m) and destroyed the town of Yungay six minutes later. More than 50,000 people were killed.

STEMMING THE FLOW

Japan has a large population and 10 per cent of the world's active volcanoes. It leads the way in mudflow control. Scientists use television monitors and other measuring instruments to detect volcanic activity. Check dams such as these are used around the very active Mt. Sakurajima. Steel and concrete slit dams, shown below, slow down and redirect flows of mud. Although the mudflows sometimes spill over the dams, people in danger have time to prepare or evacuate.

WHEN A CALDERA FORMS
During mild explosions, magma rises to the top of the volcano's main vent.

ERUPTING CALDERA
A cloud of ash and gas erupts from the caldera of Mt. Ngauruhoe in New Zealand.

THE NEXT STAGE
As the eruption increases in strength, the magma rapidly sinks back down to the top of the magma chamber.

THE CLIMAX
In Plinian or Peléean eruptions, the activity climaxes and magma sinks below the roof of the magma chamber, leaving an empty space where it once supported the roof.

• A F T E R   T H E   E V E N T •

Craters and Calderas

C raters are the funnel-shaped hollows or cavities that form at the openings or vents of volcanoes. The simplest craters occur on the top of cones and usually have a diameter of about 6/10 mile (1 km) or less. Volcanoes can also form craters at the side. Small lava lakes occur when the lava is unable to escape, and it blocks the vent like a bath plug. Calderas are very large craters formed by an explosion or massive volcanic eruption. The magma chamber empties and can no longer support the weight of the volcano and the cone collapses. Calderas are often more than 3 miles (5 km) in diameter. The world's largest caldera is at Aso, Japan, and it is 14 miles (23 km) long and 10 miles (16 km) wide. When a volcano is dormant or extinct, a caldera can fill with water to form a large lake.

KILAUEA CRATER
Lava erupts from the crater of Kilauea volcano on Hawaii.

CRATER LAKES

These lakes form when the main vents of dormant or extinct volcanoes are plugged with hardened lava or other rubble. Over many years the crater gradually fills with water from rain or snow. Shown here is Crater Lake in Oregon. This lake is a caldera that formed when the summit of Mt. Mazama collapsed more than 6,600 years ago. The small cone within the caldera is called Wizard Island.

LIFE IN A CALDERA
Pinggan Village is one of the many villages within the caldera of the extinct volcano Gunung Batur, in Bali, Indonesia.

THE COLLAPSE
Once the magma support is removed, the top collapses into the magma chamber, and more eruptions can occur on the caldera floor.

STRANGE BUT TRUE
On the Indonesian island of Flores, the volcano of Keli Mutu is well known for its different colored crater lakes. Tiwoe Noea Moeri Kooh Pai is green, Tiwoe Ata is light green and Tiwoe Ata Polo is an amazing red color.

Discover more in Volcanic Eruptions

VOLCANIC PLUG
This plug in Cameroon, West Africa, started as magma in the vent of a volcano. Over millions of years the magma cooled and hardened. The softer rocks eroded and left the plug exposed.

Volcanic Rocks and Landforms

Deep within the Earth the heat is so intense that the red-hot rock or magma is molten. This magma rises toward the surface through cracks in the crust, then cools and hardens to form igneous rocks. When these rocks cool slowly underground within the cracks, they form intrusive igneous rocks such as granite. Intrusive rocks may appear on the surface when the surrounding softer rocks erode and expose amazing landscapes with landforms such as sills, dykes and plugs. Magma that erupts at the surface as lava and cools quickly becomes extrusive igneous rock. Runny lavas produce a rock called basalt, which in large quantities can flood an area and make basalt plateaus. Thicker, stickier lava can produce pumice, volcanic glass such as obsidian, and a light-colored rock called rhyolite.

ROCK WALL
Most volcanoes are fed by magma that forces its way up through vertical cracks in the rocks. The magma can harden underground to form a wall of rock called a dike. Erosion has exposed this dike in eastern Australia, which is called the "Breadknife."

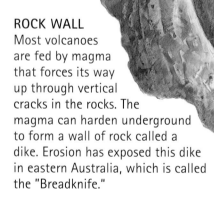

HOT SPRINGS
Hot springs form when water seeps down through rocks and is heated by magma or hot rock from below. The water then rises up towards the surface. This Japanese macaque enjoys a warm soak in one of the hot springs in northern Japan—a volcanic area near the boundaries of the Pacific and Philippine plates.

DID YOU KNOW?

Diamonds originate in the mantle under extreme heat and pressure. Diamonds, such as this one embedded in volcanic rock called kimberlite, are pushed to the surface by rising magma.

USEFUL VOLCANOES

There are many uses for volcanic rocks. Small amounts of ash can add nutrients to soil. Basalt and granite are useful building materials. The mineral sulfur grows around the vents of some active volcanoes. Sulfur is mined for use in manufacturing. It is added to rubber to make it last longer, and is also an ingredient in many explosives. Here workers carry baskets full of large sulfur crystals collected from around the vent of Kawah Ijen volcano in Java, Indonesia. This sulfur will be processed and mixed with phosphate to make a type of fertilizer.

CAPPADOCCIA

This unusual volcanic landscape formed at Cappadoccia, Turkey, from lava eruptions of the now extinct Mt. Erciyes. Wind and rain have eroded the volcanic rock into pointed formations.

P wave   S wave

Surface wave

Detecting Earthquakes

Every 30 seconds the Earth shakes slightly. Most of these tremors are recorded by sensitive instruments but are too small to be felt by humans. Earthquakes occur when there is a build-up of stress in the crust caused by plate movement at either a subduction zone or along what is called a fault line—a crack or break in the Earth's crust where rocks have shifted. The place where the rocks move or break is called the focus or point of origin. The movement sends shock waves shooting through the surrounding rocks in all directions and the ground on the surface shakes. The force of these waves depends on how deep down the focus is, the strength of the surrounding rocks and how much they move. The epicenter on the surface is directly above the focus, but the greatest damage can occur many miles away. In an earthquake, primary waves hit first, then come the secondary waves and the most destructive surface waves. Foreshocks and aftershocks can occur for some time before and after the main earthquake.

EARTHQUAKE WAVES
The energy generated by an earthquake travels in the form of waves through the surrounding rocks. This wavy line shows a typical printout, called a seismogram, of earthquake waves. Even the slightest ground tremors are recorded.

DID YOU KNOW?
Instruments detect more than 600,000 Earth tremors each year. Most earthquakes occur in the ocean crust or in areas where there are no people or buildings.

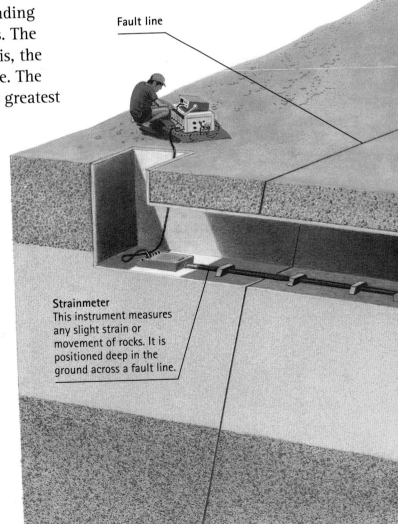

Fault line

Strainmeter
This instrument measures any slight strain or movement of rocks. It is positioned deep in the ground across a fault line.

THE FIRST SEISMOMETER
In AD 130 Zhang Heng, a Chinese astronomer, invented the first instrument for detecting earthquakes. If the Earth trembled, a bronze ball fell from the dragon's mouth into the mouth of a frog below.

ANIMALS AND EARTHQUAKES

Can animals sense the approach of an earthquake? Many people and some scientists believe they can. During the winter of 1974–75 in Haicheng, China, things were jumping. Chickens, snakes, frogs and dogs were restless. In February, instruments recorded slight Earth tremors to the north, and the order was given to evacuate more than a million people from the area. By early evening on the same day a huge earthquake devastated the region. Scientists have monitored a variety of creatures, such as catfish in Japan and beetles in California, to find out if they do have a secret sense for detecting earthquakes, but there has been no conclusive evidence.

Space-age technology
Satellites are used to help detect movements in the Earth. By bouncing a laser beam between Earth and an orbiting satellite, scientists can measure the large-scale movement of rocks.

Seismic trucks
The vibrating seismic truck uses a large metal plate to pound the Earth and produce a series of small shock waves. These waves are monitored by the nearby recorder truck. This allows scientists to map out the different rock layers of the Earth.

DETECTING AND MEASURING
Scientists monitor active earthquake areas around the world with various kinds of sensitive and highly sophisticated equipment.

NASA radio telescopes
A large satellite dish is used to pick up signals from outer space. The arrival time of the radio signals on Earth is used as a reference point to measure the movement of rocks.

Seismometer
A seismometer detects, measures and records any slight tremor in the ground at a specific location.

Borehole tiltmeter
Scientists drill holes approximately 328 ft (100 m) deep in the ground to install a borehole tiltmeter. It is used to measure a change in the tilt of the ground.

Long baseline tiltmeter
This surface tiltmeter is dozens of feet long. Each end has a container filled with liquid. A change in the water level on either side indicates a change in the tilt of the ground.

Surviving an Earthquake

When an earthquake strikes, beware of falling buildings and flying objects. To prevent building collapse and loss of life, engineers in many earthquake-prone cities follow strict rules when they repair earthquake damage or put up new structures. Many buildings are now designed to rest on reinforced concrete rafts that float when shock waves pass through. Existing buildings can be reinforced by cross-bracing walls, floors, roofs and foundations to help them withstand forces striking them from all directions. Walls and ceilings are strengthened with plywood in case of fire. Some areas have flexible gas lines that bend but do not break under pressure. Heavy furniture is bolted to walls to prevent it from flying around a room. Warning systems monitor stress in the Earth's crust, but earthquakes are still unpredictable and often much stronger than expected. In some areas, earthquake-proof buildings have collapsed.

BE PREPARED
Earthquake drills are part of the daily life of school children in Parkfield, California. Part of the San Andreas fault system lies beneath this small town.

SAFETY MEASURES
In this school, computers are bolted to tables, bookshelves and cabinets are attached to walls or fastened together. Windows are covered in transparent tape to stop them from breaking during a tremor.

WHEN THE EARTH SHAKES
An earthquake alarm is attached to the school's propane gas supply. The alarm switches off the gas automatically if a tremor above 3.5 on the Richter scale rocks the building.

TRANSAMERICA BUILDING
This rocket-shaped building in San Francisco, California, is designed to withstand an earthquake. The base is built on a concrete raft that gives extra support.

DROP!
When the teacher shouts "drop," each child crouches under the nearest desk. They link one arm around the leg of the desk to anchor it, and cover their head with both hands.

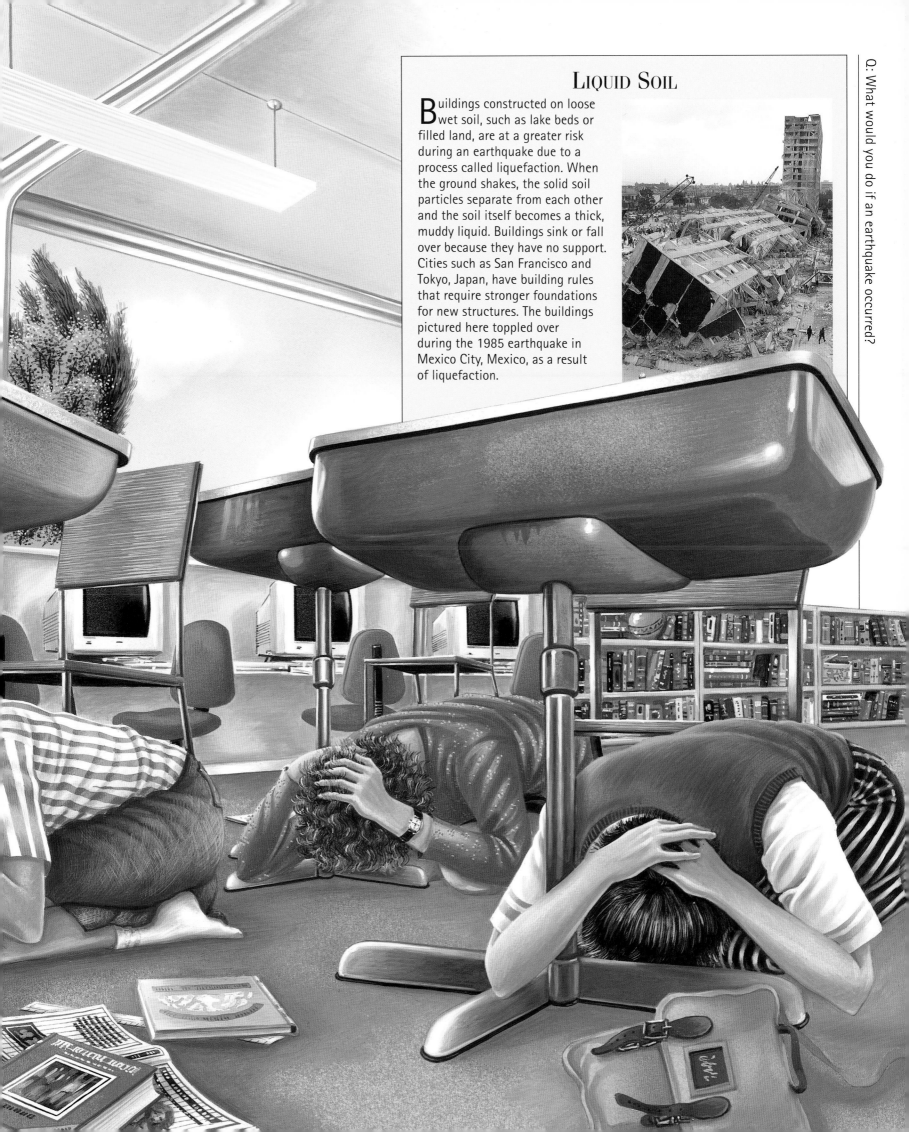

LIQUID SOIL

Buildings constructed on loose wet soil, such as lake beds or filled land, are at a greater risk during an earthquake due to a process called liquefaction. When the ground shakes, the solid soil particles separate from each other and the soil itself becomes a thick, muddy liquid. Buildings sink or fall over because they have no support. Cities such as San Francisco and Tokyo, Japan, have building rules that require stronger foundations for new structures. The buildings pictured here toppled over during the 1985 earthquake in Mexico City, Mexico, as a result of liquefaction.

TSUNAMI DAMAGE
Indonesian fishermen try to save what they can from their house, destroyed by one of the 12 tsunamis that struck East Java in June 1994.

• EARTHQUAKES •

Tsunamis and Floods

Tsunamis, huge killer waves, are caused by a jolt to the ocean floor from an earthquake, volcanic eruption or landslide. Unlike a surface wave, a tsunami is a whole column of water that reaches from the sea floor up to the surface. It can race across oceans for thousands of miles at speeds of up to 496 miles (800 km) per hour—as fast as a jet plane. Such a giant wave might stretch for hundreds of miles from crest to crest and yet remain unnoticed as it passes under ships. A sharp rise in the ocean floor near a coastline acts as a brake at the bottom of the wave and makes it stop and rush upwards in a towering wall of water that crashes onto land. The power of the wave batters and floods the coast, causing enormous damage and loss of life. Tsunamis occur most frequently in the Pacific area.

AS FAST AS A JET PLANE
The arcs of a tsunami, triggered by an earthquake in Alaska, spread quickly across the Pacific region. Seismic sea-wave detectors are in place throughout the Pacific area to measure the travel time of tsunamis and to warn populations in danger.

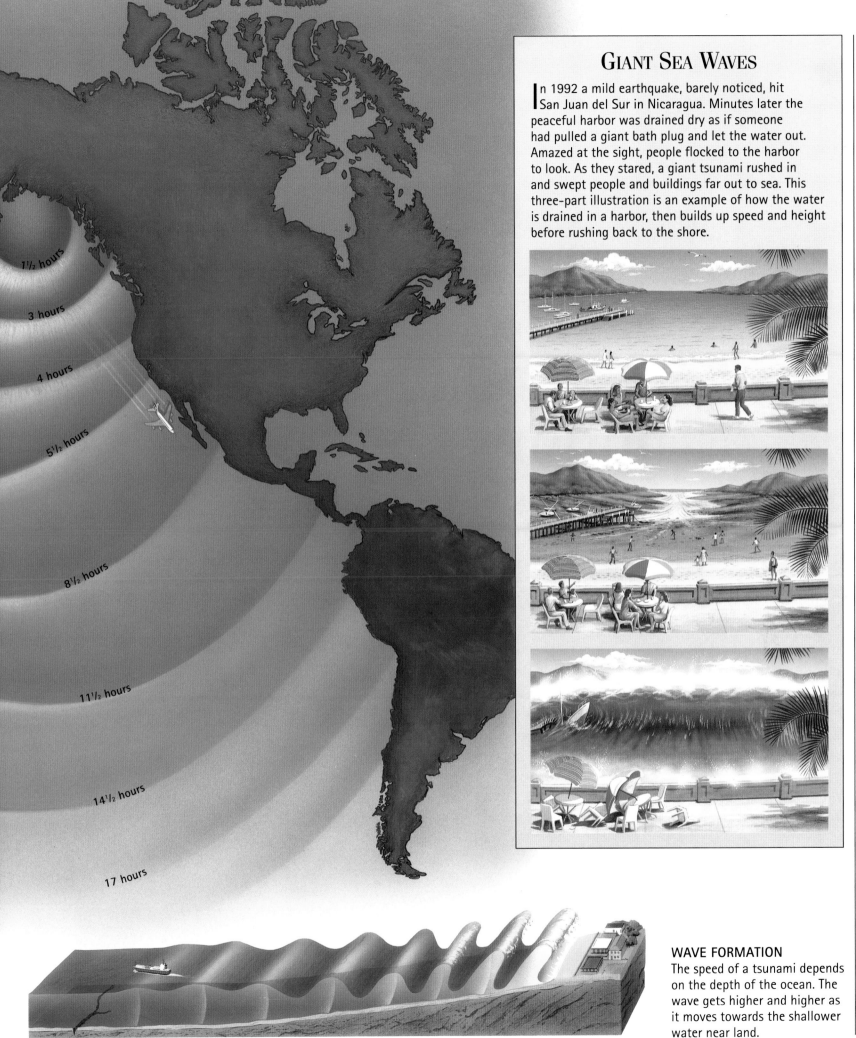

GIANT SEA WAVES

In 1992 a mild earthquake, barely noticed, hit San Juan del Sur in Nicaragua. Minutes later the peaceful harbor was drained dry as if someone had pulled a giant bath plug and let the water out. Amazed at the sight, people flocked to the harbor to look. As they stared, a giant tsunami rushed in and swept people and buildings far out to sea. This three-part illustration is an example of how the water is drained in a harbor, then builds up speed and height before rushing back to the shore.

1½ hours

3 hours

4 hours

5½ hours

8½ hours

11½ hours

14½ hours

17 hours

WAVE FORMATION
The speed of a tsunami depends on the depth of the ocean. The wave gets higher and higher as it moves towards the shallower water near land.

43

ETNA ERUPTS
A column of ash, gas and lava shoots into the air during a 1992 eruption of Mt. Etna.

THE SLOPES OF MT. ETNA
An old illustration shows the lava flow from one of the four main volcanic vents.

Mediterranean Eruptions

For more than two million years, earthquakes and volcanic eruptions have occurred in the area of the Mediterranean Sea along the boundary where the African plate meets the Eurasian plate. The Bay of Naples, in Italy, is the site of Mt. Vesuvius, which erupted violently in AD 79 and destroyed the towns of Herculaneum and Pompeii. Pliny the Younger wrote the very first account of an eruption after observing the event. Since then, Mt. Vesuvius has erupted numerous times. The last eruption was in 1944 but it is not known how long the volcano will remain dormant. Mt. Etna dominates eastern Sicily and is Europe's largest active volcano. It has been erupting periodically for more than 2,500 years and regularly destroys villages and farmland. People continue to settle on its fertile soil. The last major eruption of Mt. Etna occurred in 1992.

ON THEIR DOORSTEP
Mt. Vesuvius looms above the modern city of Naples. When will it erupt next?

DID YOU KNOW?

The 1944 eruption of Mt. Vesuvius occurred during the Second World War. Glass-sharp volcanic ash and rock fragments seriously damaged aircraft engines.

RAINING ASH

People fled the town of Herculaneum during the AD 79 eruption of Mt. Vesuvius. Some ran towards the sea and escaped in boats, but many perished when a hot surge of ash and gas covered the town.

A GREEK TRAGEDY

The beautiful ancient Greek island of Thera (today called Santorini) in the Aegean Sea was destroyed by a violent volcanic eruption 3,500 years ago. The island was home to the Minoan people, a very wealthy and advanced civilization. The eruption caused huge tsunamis and ash-falls. These swept across neighboring islands such as Crete, site of the Minoan capital of Knossos, where this vase was found. What was left of Thera was covered in more than 197 ft (60 m) of ash and pumice.

Discover more in The Digs

DISASTER SITES
This diagram compares the level of volcanic deposits that covered Herculaneum with the level that covered Pompeii.

Level of volcanic deposits at Herculaneum

Level of volcanic deposits at Pompeii

PLASTER CAST
In the 1860s, workers uncovering parts of Pompeii found holes in the volcanic rock left by the decayed bodies of the victims such as this dog. Scientists poured plaster into the holes to make models of the bodies.

• FAMOUS VOLCANOES •

The Digs

The sister cities of Pompeii and Herculaneum in Italy were destroyed when Mt. Vesuvius erupted on August 24, AD 79. Pompeii lay 5 miles (8 km) from the volcano and throughout the first afternoon and evening hot pumice, ash and rock rained down onto the crowds of fleeing people. Herculaneum, less than 3 miles (5 km) from the volcano, had only small amounts of ash-fall at first, but by midnight a pyroclastic flow of hot ash and gas followed by hot mud swept through the city, killing the residents. Early the next morning, Herculaneum was buried under 66 ft (20 m) of volcanic deposits. Another surge of ash and gas killed the remaining residents of Pompeii and buried the city under 10 ft (3 m) of volcanic deposits. Over the years archaeologists have discovered bodies, buildings and many small objects that reveal the last moments of the doomed citizens.

THE FIRST VOLCANOLOGIST

From 20 miles (32 km) away, Pliny the Younger observed the AD 79 eruption of Mt. Vesuvius. In AD 104 he described the event in two letters to his friend Tacitus, a writer and historian. This was the first recorded eyewitness report of a volcanic eruption. Pliny described such things as the Earth tremors that occurred before the eruption, the large amounts of ash and pumice, the low, hot ash flows, the many tidal waves and the total darkness of the sky. He also described a large column of ash shaped like a pine tree, which shot into the air. This type of volcanic eruption has since been named a "Plinian" eruption. Pictured here is a painting of a later eruption of Mt. Vesuvius showing some of the same details described by Pliny.

EVERYDAY ITEMS
Artifacts such as this glass drinking cup were found unbroken beneath the rubble.

RINGS ON HER FINGERS
Nearly 100 skeletons, including this one nicknamed "The Ring Lady," have been discovered in boatsheds and on the site of the ancient beach of Herculaneum. These people died while attempting to flee from the gas and ash of the eruption.

STRANGE BUT TRUE
By studying skeletons, scientists can find out a person's sex, race, height and approximate age. Bones can also reveal the type of work a person did and the kind of food they ate.

ROMAN COINS
These coins were found still safe inside a soldier's money belt.

HERCULANEUM TODAY
The ruins of the town lie 66 ft (20 m) beneath the modern city of Ercolano. Mt. Vesuvius can be seen in the background.

Discover more in Mediterranean Eruptions

DID YOU KNOW?
Although the 1815 eruption of Tambora in Indonesia was a much larger and more violent eruption, Krakatau seized the entire world's attention because of modern communication networks.

Over England
The evening sky over London dazzled onlookers with beautiful colors. Waves raised the tides in the English Channel.

Weather changes
Volcanic dust circled the globe for several years and lowered the Earth's average temperature. Hawaiians noticed a white halo around the sun.

Trinidad
On the other side of the globe, in Trinidad, the sun appeared blue.

• FAMOUS VOLCANOES •

Krakatau

In May, 1883, ash, gas and pumice erupted from a volcano on the Indonesian island of Krakatau. The island is located in an unstable area where the Indo-Australian plate subducts under the Eurasian plate. The early rumblings from the volcano were just warm-ups before the violent explosion that blew the island apart on August 27. The boom from the explosion, one of the loudest ever recorded, was heard 2,170 miles (3,500 km) away. Clouds of dust and ash rose 50 miles (80 km) into the air, circled the globe, and created many colorful sunsets around the world. As the volcano collapsed in on itself, giant waves called tsunamis rose more than 131 ft (40 m) high. These walls of water surged into 163 villages along the coastlines of Java and Sumatra, destroying them and killing almost 36,000 villagers. Floating islands of pumice endangered ships sailing in the Indian Ocean.

NEARING THE END
This nineteenth-century engraving was based on an old photograph taken in 1883, just three months before Krakatau exploded.

48

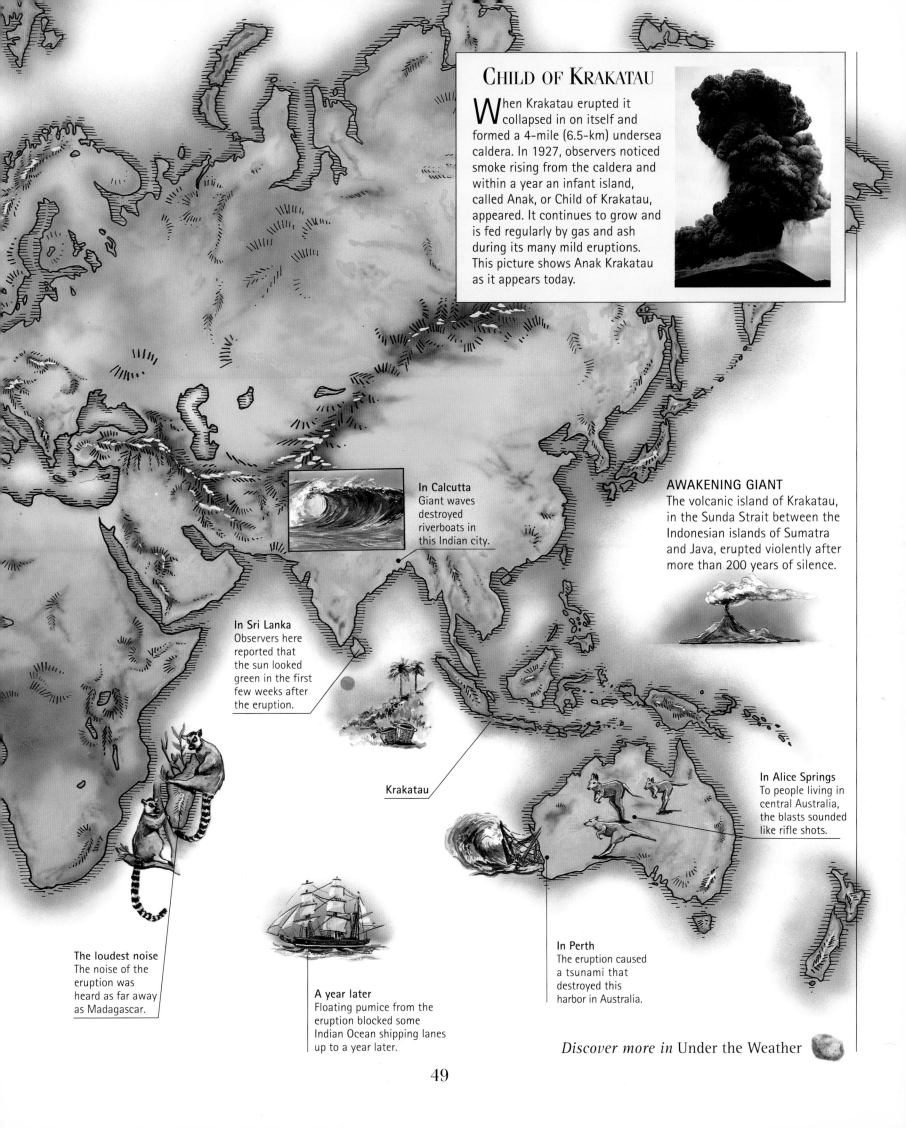

CHILD OF KRAKATAU

When Krakatau erupted it collapsed in on itself and formed a 4-mile (6.5-km) undersea caldera. In 1927, observers noticed smoke rising from the caldera and within a year an infant island, called Anak, or Child of Krakatau, appeared. It continues to grow and is fed regularly by gas and ash during its many mild eruptions. This picture shows Anak Krakatau as it appears today.

In Calcutta
Giant waves destroyed riverboats in this Indian city.

AWAKENING GIANT

The volcanic island of Krakatau, in the Sunda Strait between the Indonesian islands of Sumatra and Java, erupted violently after more than 200 years of silence.

In Sri Lanka
Observers here reported that the sun looked green in the first few weeks after the eruption.

Krakatau

In Alice Springs
To people living in central Australia, the blasts sounded like rifle shots.

The loudest noise
The noise of the eruption was heard as far away as Madagascar.

A year later
Floating pumice from the eruption blocked some Indian Ocean shipping lanes up to a year later.

In Perth
The eruption caused a tsunami that destroyed this harbor in Australia.

Discover more in Under the Weather

49

Iceland

Iceland is an island country that sits astride the northern Atlantic section of the mid-ocean ridge. The island provides scientists with an ideal place to study the ocean ridge above water. One part of Iceland is on the North American plate, which is moving westward, and the other part is on the Eurasian plate, which is moving eastward. As the island is slowly pulled in two, a rift, or large crack, is forming. Ravines and cliffs mark the edges of the two plates. Magma rising to the surface has created a series of central volcanoes separated by groups of fissures. As the area becomes more unstable, there is more earthquake and volcanic activity. Icelanders use the geothermal energy from their volcanoes for central heating, hot water and other electrical power.

DRAMATIC DISPLAY
Eldfell volcano gives a dramatic light show behind this church in the seaport town of Vestmannaeyjar.

AN ISLAND ERUPTION
In January, 1973, the seaport town of Vestmannaeyjar on Heimaey Island became the site of a new volcano called Eldfell. Most residents were evacuated, but for six months volunteers stayed behind to save what they could of the town.

Lava flow
Residents armed with fire hoses sprayed water on the advancing lava that threatened to take over the harbor. They saved the harbor but not before the lava flow added another 1 sq mile (2.6 sq km) of new land to the island.

LANDSCAPE OF FIRE

In 1783, the 3-mile (5-km) long Lakagígar fissure in southern Iceland began erupting huge fountains of lava and large amounts of gas and ash. The lava flow, one of the largest ever recorded on Earth, eventually covered more than 220 sq miles (565 sq km) of land. A deadly blue haze settled over the country and spread to parts of Europe and Asia. Nobody was killed by the lava itself, but Iceland's crops were destroyed and much of the livestock starved to death. More than 10,000 people died in the famine that followed. Since then, fissures such as the one at Krafla in northeastern Iceland have continued to erupt.

The craters of Lakagígar fissure

Krafla fissure

BACKYARD VOLCANO
The crater of Eldfell glowed red as thick lava flowed down the side of the volcano and fiery ash rained down on the abandoned houses.

BURIED IN ASH
Much of the town lay beneath a thick layer of ash. Here, volunteers clear ash from rooftops to prevent the houses from collapsing.

Mt. St. Helens

The volcano Mt. St. Helens is one of 15 in the Cascade Range of the northwest United States—an area where the Juan de Fuca plate is subducting beneath the North American plate. On March 20, 1980, a string of earthquakes northwest of the mountain peak signalled the slow awakening of the volcano, which had been dormant since 1857. A week later, a small eruption shot ash and steam into the air. Groups of scientists arrived with instruments to monitor the volcano. By early May, a bulge developed on the cone. This indicated magma rising in the volcano's vent. The bulge grew bigger each day until a violent explosion, probably triggered by another earthquake, blew out the northern side of the mountain on May 18. This caused an enormous landslide that devastated an area of 234 sq miles (600 sq km) and triggered mudflows and floods.

BEFORE
In early 1980, the beautiful snow-capped peak of Mt. St. Helens was surrounded by forests and lakes.

AND AFTER
The north side of the nearly perfect cone blew apart in minutes, causing one of the largest volcanic landslides ever recorded.

PLINIAN PLUME
Minutes after the first explosion a second eruption produced a large Plinian column of ash and gas that rose to a height of 12 miles (20 km). This phase of the volcanic eruption continued for nine hours.

LIKE MATCHSTICKS
More than six million trees were uprooted or flattened by rock blasted from the volcano. After a massive salvage operation to clear the logs, seedlings were planted to replace the forests.

MUDFLOWS
Thick, sticky mud caused by melting snow and ice sped down the North Toutle River Valley into communities below.

SWEEPING ASH

Millions of tons of ash shot 15 miles (25 km) into the atmosphere and the falling ash spread more than 930 miles (1,500 km) to the east. Ash fell like black snow in parts of Montana, Idaho, Oregon and Washington and covered streets, cars and buildings. Cats and dogs downwind from the eruption turned pale grey from the ash that floated from the sky. But ash does not melt like snow, and it had to be cleared. Most ended up in landfills.

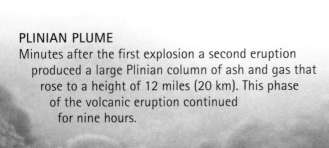

CITY IN RUINS

The earthquake struck at midday when many households were preparing their meals on hibachis—a type of open stove. As the buildings collapsed they caught fire and flames swept quickly through the city, killing thousands of people. All but one section of Tokyo was damaged by fire, and the business district was virtually destroyed.

WORLDWIDE RESPONSE

News of the devastating earthquake flashed around the world, and many countries rushed to Japan's aid with relief supplies.

• FAMOUS EARTHQUAKES •

The Great Kanto Earthquake

The Great Kanto Earthquake shook Japan on September 1, 1923. The earthquake originated beneath Sagami Bay, Yokohama, 50 miles (80 km) south of the capital, Tokyo. The power of the earthquake registered a massive 8.3 on the Richter scale, and the ground shook for nearly five minutes. A staggering 100,000 people died, and more than 300,000 buildings were destroyed. The earthquake was soon followed by a killer tsunami, which swept people and their homes far out to sea. More deaths were caused by the many fires that broke out among the paper and wood houses. These building materials had been specially chosen to make the homes safer in an earthquake, but instead they provided fuel for the raging flames. A second major tremor blasted the area 24 hours later, and minor aftershocks followed in the next few days.

JAPANESE QUAKES

Japan is situated where the Philippine plate and the Pacific plate are subducting under the Eurasian plate. This makes Japan the site of frequent volcanic eruptions, earthquakes and tsunamis. People in Japan feel Earth tremors every few weeks. Cities such as Tokyo have disaster teams ready to jump into action. Many people have prepared emergency supply kits with food, water and medicine, and most take part in earthquake drills. In October, 1994, a major earthquake estimated at 7.9 on the Richter scale occurred in the ocean crust off Hokkaido, the northernmost island in Japan, causing many buildings to collapse (above). Three months later an earthquake estimated at 6.9 on the Richter scale shattered the city of Kobe. More than 5,000 people died.

REDUCED TO RUBBLE
So great was the force of the earthquake that the floor of Sagami Bay split. At the seaport of Yokohama, south of Tokyo, most buildings were destroyed as well as the harbor and port facilities.

Discover more in Quake!

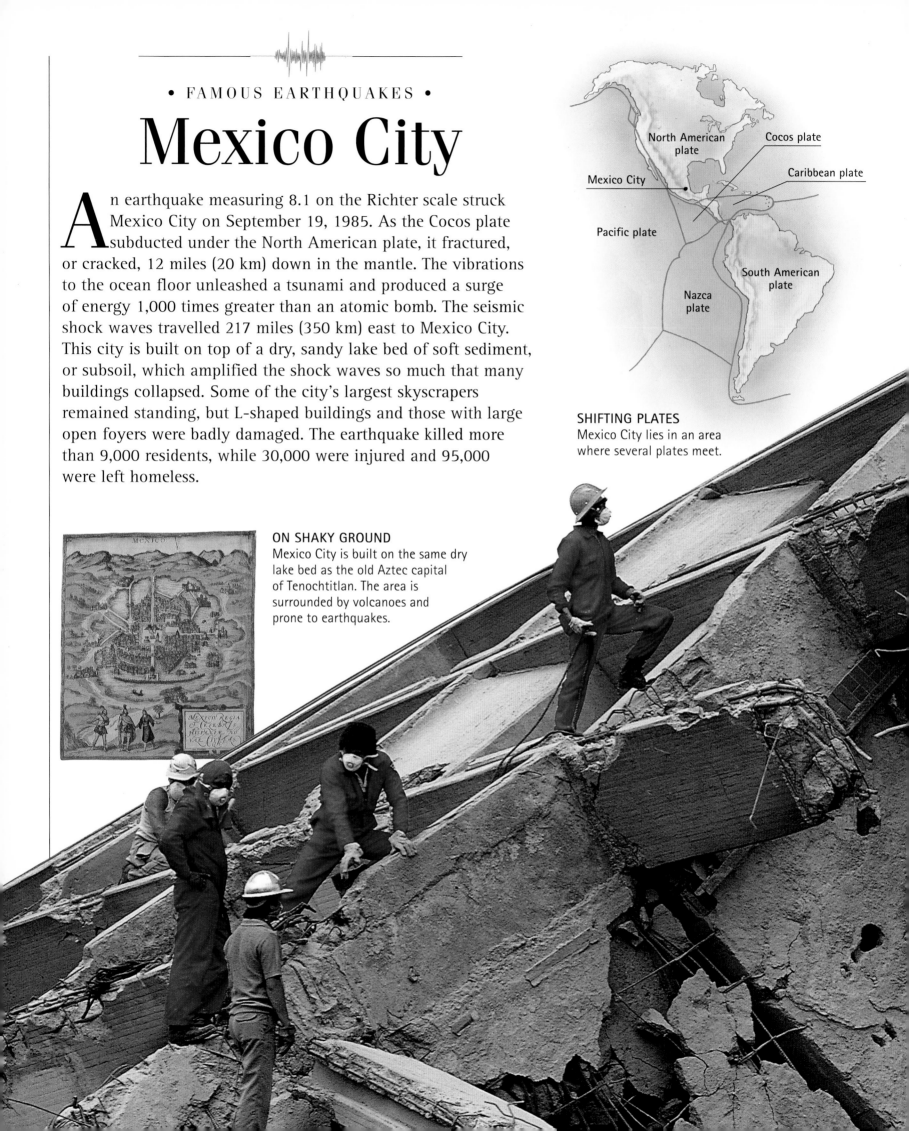

Mexico City

An earthquake measuring 8.1 on the Richter scale struck Mexico City on September 19, 1985. As the Cocos plate subducted under the North American plate, it fractured, or cracked, 12 miles (20 km) down in the mantle. The vibrations to the ocean floor unleashed a tsunami and produced a surge of energy 1,000 times greater than an atomic bomb. The seismic shock waves travelled 217 miles (350 km) east to Mexico City. This city is built on top of a dry, sandy lake bed of soft sediment, or subsoil, which amplified the shock waves so much that many buildings collapsed. Some of the city's largest skyscrapers remained standing, but L-shaped buildings and those with large open foyers were badly damaged. The earthquake killed more than 9,000 residents, while 30,000 were injured and 95,000 were left homeless.

SHIFTING PLATES
Mexico City lies in an area where several plates meet.

North American plate

Cocos plate

Mexico City

Caribbean plate

Pacific plate

South American plate

Nazca plate

ON SHAKY GROUND
Mexico City is built on the same dry lake bed as the old Aztec capital of Tenochtitlan. The area is surrounded by volcanoes and prone to earthquakes.

SIGNS OF LIFE
Teams of rescue workers searched carefully through the rubble of destroyed buildings looking for survivors. They listened for sounds of life in the wreckage. Rescuers worked nonstop for days after the earthquake and saved more than 4,000 lives.

A CLASH OF FOUR PLATES
The Nazca, Cocos, South American and Caribbean plates meet and interact along the eastern section of the Pacific Ring of Fire. Plate movement triggers a large number of earthquakes and volcanoes in some areas of North America, Central America and South America. Pictured here is Arenal volcano in Costa Rica.

STRANGE BUT TRUE
A four-day-old baby boy survived for nine days buried under the rubble of a hospital. Here, the miracle baby is lifted to safety by rescue workers.

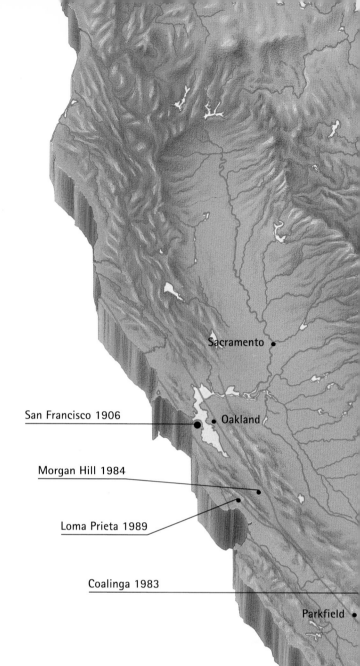

Californian Quakes

Many of the world's earthquakes occur along an edge where two lithospheric plates meet. The state of California straddles two such plates. Most of the state sits on the North American plate, which is moving very slowly. The Pacific plate, with the rest of the state, is grinding past the North American plate more quickly, and moving northwest. The grating movement of the two plates has made a weblike series of faults and cracks in the crust where earthquakes can occur. The San Andreas Fault is the most famous fault in California and slashes through the state for 682 miles (1,100 km). From time to time, the rock breaks and moves along a section of the fault, and this can trigger an earthquake. Scientists record more than 20,000 Earth tremors in California every year, although most are slight and detected only by sensitive instruments.

Sacramento

San Francisco 1906

Oakland

Morgan Hill 1984

Loma Prieta 1989

Coalinga 1983

Parkfield

STRANDED
Many commuters were trapped when sections of the California freeway system collapsed during the Loma Prieta earthquake in 1989.

DID YOU KNOW?
Los Angeles sits on the Pacific plate. San Francisco sits on the North American plate. Perhaps in a million years or so they will meet.

THE STREETS OF SAN FRANCISCO
A major earthquake could strike California at any time. Movement along the San Andreas fault system could cause massive destruction in cities such as San Francisco and Los Angeles. Oil refineries, chemical and atomic plants, office towers, schools, hospitals, freeways, sports arenas, amusement parks and residential areas would all be affected.

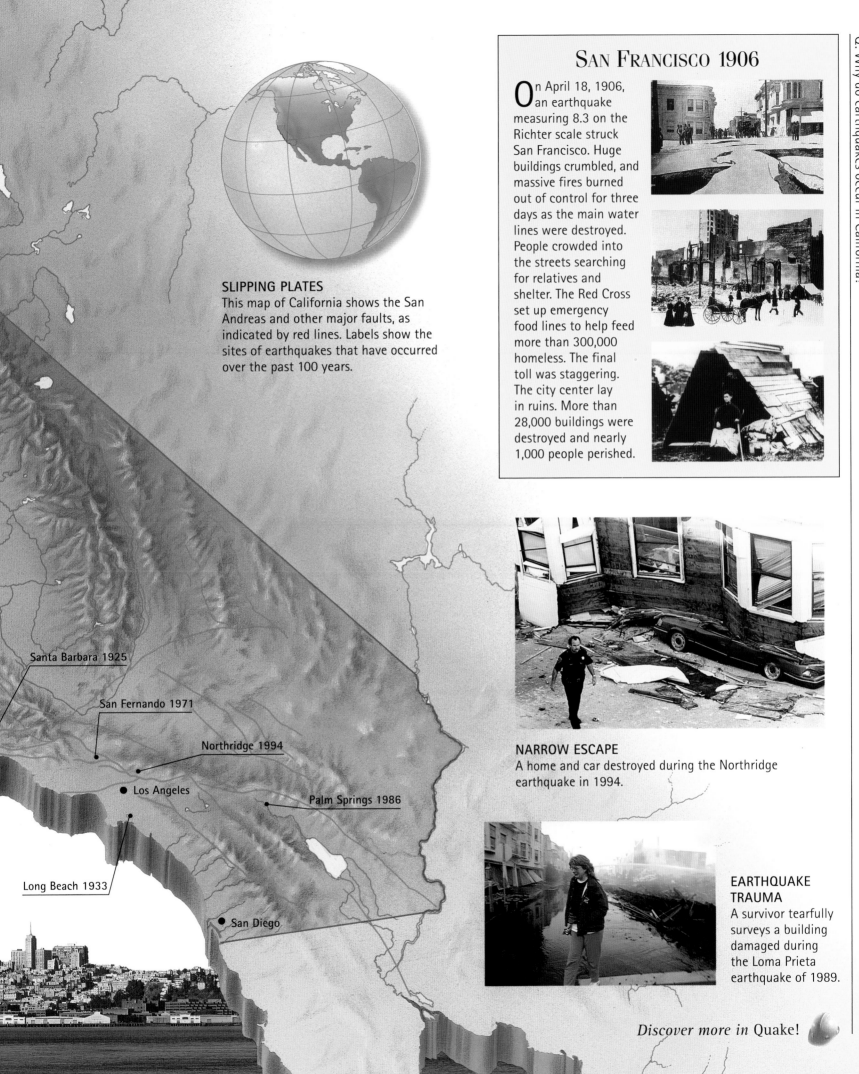

SLIPPING PLATES
This map of California shows the San Andreas and other major faults, as indicated by red lines. Labels show the sites of earthquakes that have occurred over the past 100 years.

Santa Barbara 1925

San Fernando 1971

Northridge 1994

• Los Angeles

Palm Springs 1986

Long Beach 1933

• San Diego

SAN FRANCISCO 1906
On April 18, 1906, an earthquake measuring 8.3 on the Richter scale struck San Francisco. Huge buildings crumbled, and massive fires burned out of control for three days as the main water lines were destroyed. People crowded into the streets searching for relatives and shelter. The Red Cross set up emergency food lines to help feed more than 300,000 homeless. The final toll was staggering. The city center lay in ruins. More than 28,000 buildings were destroyed and nearly 1,000 people perished.

NARROW ESCAPE
A home and car destroyed during the Northridge earthquake in 1994.

EARTHQUAKE TRAUMA
A survivor tearfully surveys a building damaged during the Loma Prieta earthquake of 1989.

Discover more in Quake!

More about Volcanic Eruptions

AD 186 Taupo, New Zealand

One of the largest volcanic eruptions in history occurred in Taupo in the North Island of New Zealand. Although quiet for more than 1,800 years, the volcano is still considered to be active.

AD 79 Mt. Vesuvius, Italy

The cities of Pompeii and Herculaneum were destroyed in AD 79 when Mt. Vesuvius erupted. Until then, people did not know that the mountain was a volcano—it had been silent for more than 300 years.

1783 Lakagigar, Iceland

Lakagigar fissure erupted one of the largest amounts of lava in history. The fissure also erupted huge amounts of ash and poisonous gases. A blue haze settled over parts of Europe. Benjamin Franklin, living in France at the time, correctly blamed the unusually cold summer on the eruption in Iceland.

1815 Tambora, Indonesia

The eruption of Tambora is considered to be the most destructive volcanic explosion ever. More than 10,000 people died during the eruption and a further 82,000 people died of disease and starvation after the event.

1991 Mt. Pinatubo, Philippines

1902 Mt. Pelée, Martinique

1902 Mt. Pelée, Martinique

After signs of increased volcanic activity, Mt. Pelée exploded violently, destroying the beautiful city of St. Pierre. A glowing cloud of gas and ash raced down the mountain towards the city below. More than 28,000 people perished in less than a minute. The only survivor was a prisoner held in a tiny dungeon.

1980 Mt. St. Helens, United States

For people living close by, the sound from the massive explosion of Mt. St. Helens was muffled by vegetation and a huge cloud of ash and dust. People living hundreds of miles away, however, heard the explosion because the sound bounced off layers in the Earth's outer atmosphere.

1982 El Chichon, Mexico

More than 3,500 people were killed in this eruption. So much ash shot into the sky that it remained dark for 44 hours.

1991 Unzen, Japan

The 1991 eruption was predicted by scientists, and most people were evacuated in time. Many of the 38 people who perished in this explosion were geologists studying the eruption and journalists reporting it.

1991 Mt. Pinatubo, Philippines

After more than 600 years, Mt. Pinatubo erupted. Large amounts of ash exploded into the atmosphere and fell over a wide area. People sifting through the ash found what they believed to be diamonds. The rocks were actually quartz crystals formed by the hardening of magma inside the volcano.

1994 Rabaul, Papua New Guinea

1994 Rabaul, Papua New Guinea

The 1994 eruption was the sixth to occur in the past 200 years. Due to a successful evacuation there were very few deaths. The city was covered in a 3-ft (1-m) layer of ash, and large slabs of pumice filled the harbor.

More about Earthquakes

1755 Lisbon, Portugal

1755 Lisbon, Portugal

This wealthy merchant city was destroyed by an earthquake estimated by later seismologists to be 8.7 on the Richter scale. Buildings collapsed, tsunamis pounded the waterfront and fires burned for six days. The damage on the North African coast was so heavy that many people thought there were two earthquakes. The Lisbon earthquake was the first to be studied by scientists.

1897 Assam, India

The Assam earthquake, with a magnitude of 8.7, is one of the largest ever recorded. For the first time instruments confirmed the three types of earthquake waves.

1960 Santiago, Chile

A series of earthquakes killed more than 5,000 people. The surface waves produced were so powerful that they were still being recorded on seismographs 60 hours after the actual earthquake.

1964 Alaska, United States

The earthquake measuring between 8.3 and 8.6 originated 80 miles (129 km) east of the city of Anchorage. The ground shook for nearly seven minutes. Massive damage occurred in the heavily populated south-central area, and surface waves reshaped the coastline. Large cracks opened up in the ground, and landsliding was common. Tsunamis raced across the Pacific Ocean as far south as Antarctica.

1976 Tangshan, China

The earthquake occurred in a heavily populated area of China 37 miles (60 km) southeast of Beijing. With a magnitude of between 7.8 and 8.2, the earthquake was the most devastating to hit China in four centuries. The earthquake lasted 23 seconds but was followed by more than 125 aftershocks within 48 hours of the first tremors. The death toll was staggering. About 242,000 people were killed and more than 150,000 injured.

1988 Spitak, Armenia

With a magnitude of 6.9, the Armenian earthquake completely destroyed the town of Spitak, and nearly every building in the cities of Kirovakan and Leninakan collapsed. Thousands were trapped in the rubble. More than 25,000 people died, but miraculously, 15,000 survivors were rescued.

1989 Loma Prieta, United States

A segment of the San Andreas Fault moved and triggered a magnitude 7.1 earthquake in California. Much of the damage in the San Francisco area occurred to buildings constructed on the soft sediment of landfilled areas. Ironically, some of the landfill material used in the area was rubble cleared from the 1906 San Francisco earthquake.

1995 Kobe, Japan

More than 5,000 people died and 200,000 were left homeless in one of Japan's worst earthquakes. In 30 seconds, a devastating earthquake destroyed the city of Kobe and the surrounding villages. Broken gas mains caused fires, which swept through the streets and the tile-roofed wooden houses. Firefighters were unable to stop the flames from spreading—water mains were broken and useless. Most people were still asleep in their beds, but many early morning commuters were trapped or killed when expressways collapsed.

1988 Spitak, Armenia

Glossary

Pyroclastic rocks

Alfred Wegener

The first seismometer

Sulphur miners

Dante the robot

aa Lava that hardens with a rough, broken surface.

active volcano A volcano that can erupt at any time.

aftershock A tremor that occurs after the main shaking of an earthquake has passed.

ash Small fragments of rock and lava blown out of a volcano during an eruption.

asthenosphere The soft, squishy section of the Earth's mantle.

avalanche A mass of snow, ice or rock that breaks off from a high ledge and slides down a steep slope, picking up more material along the way. It is sometimes triggered by volcanic or earthquake activity.

basalt An extrusive igneous rock formed when runny lava cools and becomes solid.

black smoker A volcanic hot spring emerging from an active spreading ridge on the ocean floor.

caldera A crater usually more than 3 miles (5 km) in diameter formed by an explosion or powerful volcanic eruption.

continent One of the seven main land masses of the globe: Europe, Asia, Africa, North America, South America, Australia, Antarctica.

continental drift A theory proposed by Alfred Wegener whereby the continents were once joined together as one land mass, and then, over millions of years, drifted apart.

convection currents A form of motion produced by heat in the mantle. Hot rock moves up and cold rock sinks. This provides the power to move the layers of rock within the Earth and the giant lithospheric plates across the surface of the Earth.

crater A funnel-shaped opening at the top of a volcano. Craters usually have a diameter of 6/10 mile (1 km) or less.

crater lake The body of water that gathers in the volcano's crater when lava cools and blocks the vent.

crust The outer layer of the Earth.

dormant volcano A volcano that is not currently active but could erupt again.

epicenter The place on the Earth's surface that is directly above an earthquake's focus or starting point.

extinct volcano A volcano unlikely to erupt again.

extrusive rock Lava that cools and hardens quickly on the surface.

fault A crack or break in the Earth's crust where rocks have shifted.

focus The place under the Earth's surface where an earthquake's shock waves start.

foreshock A tremor that occurs before the main shock waves of an earthquake begin.

geyser A hot spring that boils and erupts hot water and steam.

Gondwana A large continent, once part of Pangaea, which included today's continents of South America, Africa, India, Australia, Antarctica and small parts of other continents.

granite An intrusive igneous rock with large crystals of quartz.

hotspot volcano A volcano that forms in the middle of a plate, above a source of magma.

hot spring A pool or spring that forms when water seeps down through rocks, is heated by magma or hot rock and then rises to the surface.

igneous rock Rock that forms when magma cools and hardens.

inner core The solid ball of iron and nickel at the center of the Earth.

intrusive rock Magma that cools and hardens slowly within the crust.

island arc A volcanic island chain that forms when magma rises from a subduction zone.

lahar A lethal mudflow often triggered by a volcano or an earthquake.

Laurasia A large continent, once part of Pangaea, which included today's continents of North America, Europe and Asia and the island of Greenland.

lava Magma that erupts at the surface of the Earth.

liquefaction A process that occurs during an earthquake when poorly consolidated or loose sand, mud and water are shaken and become liquid rather than solid. Buildings built on soil of this type can collapse because they have no support.

lithosphere The two layers of solid rock, consisting of the upper mantle and the crust, which lie above the asthenosphere.

lithospheric plate One of the slabs of the Earth's outermost part, the lithosphere.

magma Molten rock inside the Earth.

magma chamber A reservoir, or pocket, of magma in the crust.

mantle The layer of the Earth between the crust and the outer core. The mantle has three sections: the solid lower mantle, the squishy asthenosphere and the solid upper mantle.

Mercalli scale A scale that measures the intensity or amount of shaking that occurs during an earthquake. It is expressed in Roman numerals.

mid-ocean ridge A huge mountain range that snakes across the ocean floor at the boundaries of the plates where they move apart.

mudflow A fast-moving stream of ash and water caused by the eruption of an explosive volcano or an earthquake. Also called a lahar.

normal fault A type of fault where the ground cracks as rocks are pulled apart. One side slides down to a lower level.

obsidian A dark, glassy volcanic rock that forms when thick, sticky lava cools rapidly.

outer core The liquid layer of iron and nickel surrounding the inner core.

pahoehoe A fast-flowing lava that cools to form a smooth, ropelike surface.

Pangaea A supercontinent that included today's continents in one land mass.

pillow lava Lava that erupts in water, such as along the mid-ocean ridge.

plateau An area of level high ground.

primary waves The first earthquake waves to hit an area.

pumice A volcanic rock formed when frothy lava cools and hardens. The bubbles of air trapped inside make it so light that it can float in water.

pyroclastic flow A rapidly flowing hot cloud of gas and ash blown out of the mouth of a volcano.

Rescue workers

reverse fault A fault where the ground cracks as rocks are pushed together. One side slides up and over the other side to a higher level. Sometimes called a thrust fault.

rhyolite A light-colored igneous rock formed from thick, sticky lava.

Richter scale A scale that measures the amount, or magnitude, of energy released by an earthquake. It is expressed in Arabic numbers.

Plaster cast from Pompeii

ridge A long mountain.

rift The crack or valley that forms when two plates with ocean crust move apart.

Ring of Fire The area along the edges of the Pacific Ocean where many of the world's earthquakes and volcanoes occur.

secondary waves The second round of earthquake waves to hit an area.

seismic activity Any of the effects, usually Earth tremors, caused by an earthquake.

seismologist A scientist who studies earthquakes.

The "Breadknife," Australia

shock waves The energy that is generated by an earthquake and travels in the form of waves through the surrounding rocks.

silica A substance that appears as quartz, sand, flint and agate.

spreading ridge A place on the ocean floor where magma cools and hardens in a rift and adds new strips of crust to the plates.

strike-slip fault A fault where rocks break and a block of land moves sideways.

Twinned pyroxene crystals

subduction The process of one plate slowly diving beneath another. Plate is destroyed at a subduction zone.

surface waves The third and most destructive round of earthquake waves to hit an area.

tsunami A huge killer wave that reaches from the sea floor up to the surface, and speeds across the ocean before it crashes onto land.

The goddess Pelé

volcanologist A scientist who studies volcanoes.

Index

Picture Credits

(t=top, b=bottom, l=left, r=right, c=center, i=icon, F=front, C=cover, B=back, Bg=background)
Art Resource, 47tr (Borommeo). Auscape, 23tc (Explorer/K. Krafft), 15tr (J. Foott), 31tr (F. Gohier), 6/7c, 14br, 15tl, 24/25c, 27cr, 53tr (M. Krafft), 32br, 63cr (W. Lawler). David Austen, 33tr, 62cbl. Austral International, 59tcr, 32tl (Colorific!), 58cl (IME - Sipa Press/K. Levine), 29tr (Rex Features), 37tr, 38tr, 59tr (Sipa-Press), 59br (Sygma/J.P. Forden), 59bcr (Sygma/L. Francis Jr, The Fresno Bee), 59cr (Topham Picture Library), 41tr (Nik Wheeler). Australian Museum, 33tl (J. Fields). Australian Picture Library, 44cl (Agence Vandystadt/G. Planchenault), 58/59b (A. Bartel), 60bl. (Reuters), 22br, 42tl, 61br, (Reuters/Bettman), 29cr (Zefa/W. Janoud), 40bl. Black Star, 49tr (J. Delay), 52/53c (J. Mason), 52bl (R. Perry). The Bridgeman Art Library, 44bl, 47tc (Phillips, The International Fine Art Auctioneers). British Museum, 17cr, 63br. Bruce Coleman Ltd, 4bl, 32bl (S. Kaufman). Bruce Coleman, Inc., 53cr (J. Balog). Earth Images, 53br (B. Thompson). Fairfax Photo Library, 13tr, 60cr (R. Stevens). Fratelli Alinari, 16cl. Gamma Liaison, 28bl (A. Suau). Fraser Goff, 52cl (J. Hughes), 25br, 25cr. The Granger Collection, 8br, 24tl, 44c, 48br, 54tr,

55tl, 61tl, 62tcl. Icelandic Photo and Press Service, 51tc (S. Jonasson), 11br (G. Palsson), 50tr, 51tr (M. Wibe Lund). The Image Bank, 39tl (J.H. Carmichael), 38cl (G.L. Kallio), 20cl (L.J. Pierrce). Landform Slides, 31c, 47br. Mary Evans Picture Library, 54bl (Le Petit Journal). Megapress (Muroran Civil Engineering Office, Hokkaido Government), 29br. Minden Pictures, 20tl (F. Lanting). Mirror Syndication International, 56cl (British Museum/PCC/ Aldus). NASA, 24bl, 62bl. National Archaeological Museum of Athens, 45br. National Geographic Society, 46/47c, 47c (O.L. Mazzatenta). Natural History Photographic Agency, 44bc (A. Nardi). Pacific Stock, 30br (J. Carini). The Photo Library, Sydney, 57tr (G. Dimijian), 19tr (A. Evrard), 27tr (NASA/ Science Photo Library), 55tr (Sipa Press), 30tl (R. Smith), 21bcr (TSI/G.B. Lewis). Photo Researchers, 56/57c (F. Gohier). Robert Harding Picture Library, 21br (A.C. Waltham). Roger-Viollet, 55bc, 55cr, 55cl (Collection VIOLLET). The Science Museum, London 34bl, 62cl (Science & Society Picture Library). John S. Shelton, 9br. Sonia Halliday Photographs, 46cl, 63tcr. Sporting Pix/Popperfoto, 54tl. Tate Gallery, London, 27br (Cat. no. N00499). Topham Picturepoint, 21tcr.

Illustration Credits

Andrew Beckett/Garden Studio, 28/29c, 28t, 50/51c. Sian Frances/ Garden Studio, 5br, 40/41c, 57br. Mike Gorman, 18/19c, 18l, 34/39c, 34t, 46tl. Peter Kesteven/Garden Studio 44/45c. Mike Lamble, 32/33c. Kevin O'Donnell, 43r. Evert Ploeg, 48/49c. Oliver Rennert, 6tl, 8/9tc, 8l, 8tc, 9bl, 12/13c, 30/31c, 42/43c. Oliver Rennert and Ray Sim, 13cr, 14tr. John Richards, 2, 3, 4/5b, 35–37c, 35bc, 35tl, 37br, 38br, 63tr. Trevor Ruth, 10/11c, 11cr, 14/15c, 20/21c. Stephen Seymour/Bernard Thornton Artists, UK, 5tr, 22/23c, 22cl, 23tr, 62tl. Ray Sim, 16tl, 56tr. Kevin Stead, 26/27c, 26tl. Steve Trevaskis, 4tl, 16/17c, 17tr, 63bcr. Rod Westblade, 1, 29br, 43b, 58/59c, 59tc, endpapers, icons.

Cover Credits

Auscape, Bg (M. Krafft). Austral International, FCc (IME - Sipa Press / Ken Levine). The Photo Library, Sydney, FCb (David Hardy, Science Photo Library). Oliver Rennert, BCbr. Stephen Seymour/Bernard Thornton Artists, UK, BCtl.

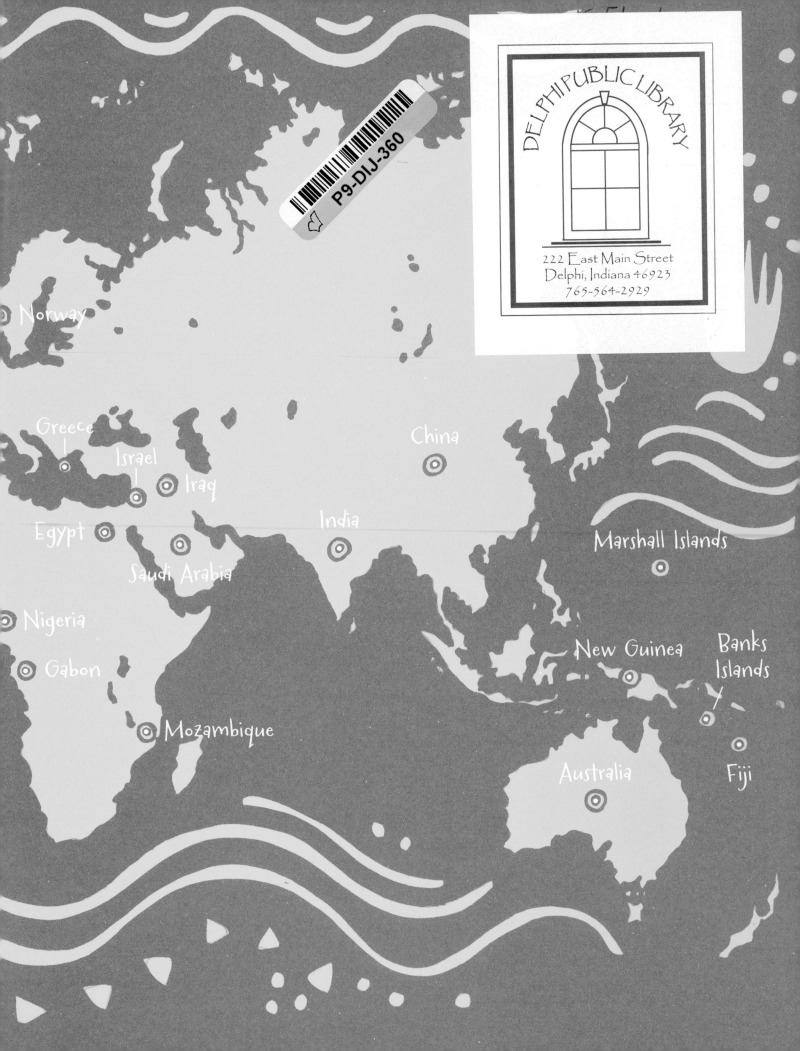

Norway

Greece

Israel

Iraq

Egypt

Saudi Arabia

China

India

Marshall Islands

Nigeria

Gabon

New Guinea

Banks Islands

Mozambique

Australia

Fiji

Author's Note

Ever since humans could speak, they've been asking, "How did the world begin?" We're still asking. Some of the newest answers resemble some of the oldest. Today's big bang theory proposes that the whole universe came out of a microscopic speck of matter, much like the myths in which the solar system was packed inside an egg. The cycles of creation and destruction in Mexican and Hindu accounts are reminiscent of geology's descriptions of the comings and goings of continents and oceans.

To read creation stories in full, I recommend these collections:
In the Beginning: Creation Stories from Around the World by Virginia Hamilton
Creation: Read-Aloud Stories from Many Lands by Ann Pilling
The Four Corners of the Sky: Creation Stories and Cosmologies from Around the World by Steve Zeitlin

In addition to the above, I drew on many works for adults and am especially grateful to Barbara C. Sproul for her book, *Primal Myths: Creation Myths Around the World*.

Henry Holt and Company, LLC
Publishers since 1866
175 Fifth Avenue
New York, New York 10010
mackids.com

Library of Congress Cataloging-in-Publication Data
Names: Fleischman, Paul, author. | Paschkis, Julie, illustrator.
Title: First light, first life / Paul Fleischman ; illustrated by Julie Paschkis.
Description: First Edition. | New York : Henry Holt Company, 2016.
Identifiers: LCCN 2015030948 | ISBN 9781627791014 (hardback)
Subjects: LCSH: Creation—Mythology—Juvenile literature. | Beginning—Juvenile literature. |
BISAC: JUVENILE FICTION / Fairy Tales & Folklore / Adaptations. |
JUVENILE FICTION / Fairy Tales & Folklore / Country & Ethnic. | JUVENILE FICTION / People & Places / General.
Classification: LCC BL325.C7 F55 2016 | DDC 202/.4—dc23
LC record available at http://lccn.loc.gov/2015030948

Our books may be purchased in bulk for promotional, educational, or business use.
Please contact your local bookseller or the Macmillan Corporate and Premium Sales Department at
(800) 221-7945 ext. 5442 or by e-mail at MacmillanSpecialMarkets@macmillan.com.

First Edition—2016 / Designed by Liz Dresner
The artist used gouache on paper to create the illustrations in this book.
Printed in China by Toppan Leefung Printing Ltd., Dongguan City, Guangdong Province
1   3   5   7   9   10   8   6   4   2

In the beginning, there
was only darkness.

CHINA

In the beginning, there was only water.

FIJI

In the beginning, there was fire and ice.

NORWAY

MALI

In the beginning, there was a single drop of milk.

Nothing existed but the first god.
How did he come to be? He created
himself by speaking his own name.

EGYPT

GREECE

The goddess of all things produced an egg. It floated on the water with a serpent coiled around it for protection. When it hatched, out came the sun and the planets, the moon and the earth.

ISRAEL

God said, "Let there be light,"
and light appeared.

ALASKA

There was no light on Earth.
Then Raven stole a ball of light and
dropped pieces of it so people could see.

BANKS ISLANDS

Night didn't exist until the god Quat brought it from another island. He released it from his hands and the sky went dark. Then Quat showed his brothers how to make beds from coconut fronds and how to lie down and sleep.

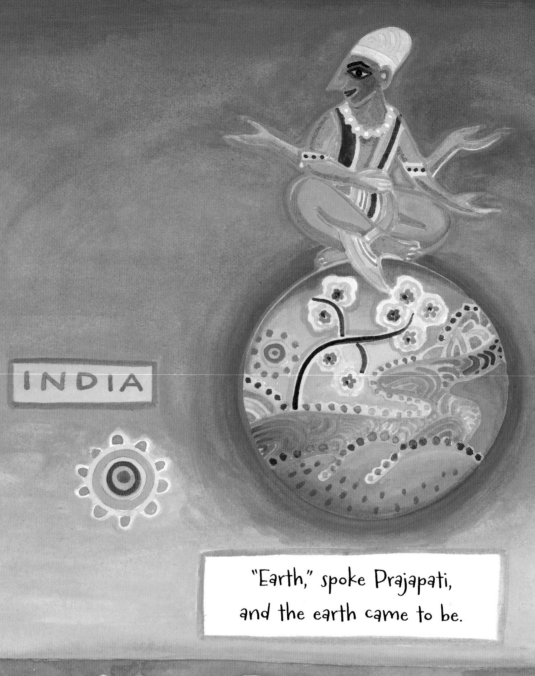

INDIA

"Earth," spoke Prajapati,
and the earth came to be.

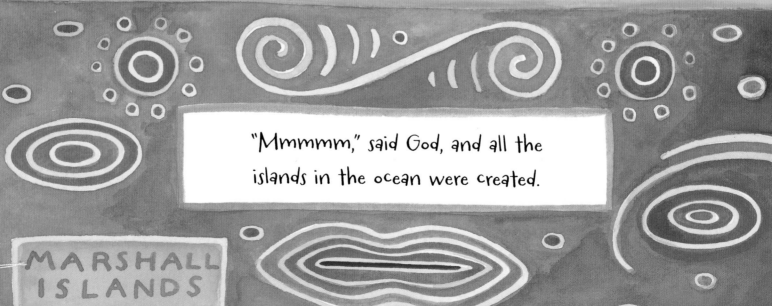

"Mmmmm," said God, and all the
islands in the ocean were created.

MARSHALL
ISLANDS

NIGERIA

All was water. Then Obatala climbed down from the sky with a snail shell filled with earth, the first dry land.

"Swim all the way down to the bottom of the water," Inktonmi commanded the animals, "and bring up some earth." Many failed. Then Muskrat came up with a tiny bit in his claws. From this, Inktonmi created the earth.

SOUTH DAKOTA

The tears of the creator Phan-Ku became rivers. His bones became rocks. His hair became trees and plants.

CHINA

The Sun Mother went into a cave.
She woke the insects waiting there
and led them out. She entered
another cave and woke the lizards.
Then the frogs. Then the birds.

AUSTRALIA

The tears of the creator Phan-Ku became rivers. His bones became rocks. His hair became trees and plants.

CHINA

The Sun Mother went into a cave. She woke the insects waiting there and led them out. She entered another cave and woke the lizards. Then the frogs. Then the birds.

AUSTRALIA

ALASKA

Raven formed animals out of mud. Then he flapped his wings, breathing life into them.

"I will make people," said the sun god, Ra.
From his own tears the first humans were born.

BANKS ISLANDS

Quat made the first humans out of wood. They lay there, lifeless. "Bring me my drum," he said. When he beat it, the humans began dancing and came to life.

Spider Woman mixed four earths together—black, white, red, and yellow. She covered them with her cape and sang the creation song over them. When she pulled back her cape, the first humans were there.

ARIZONA

BRAZIL

Karusakaibo made the world, but there were no humans. "People are living under the earth," Opossum told him. The two of them made a cotton rope, lowered it into a hole, and waited. Then up climbed the first person.

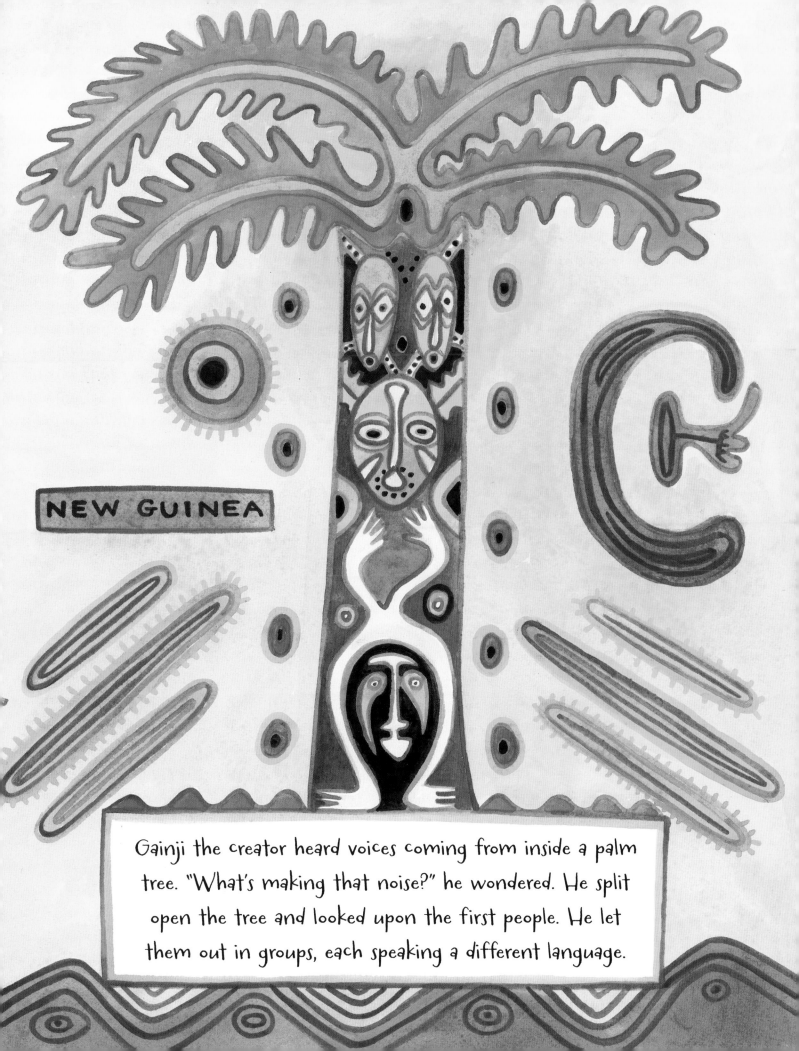

NEW GUINEA

Gainji the creator heard voices coming from inside a palm tree. "What's making that noise?" he wondered. He split open the tree and looked upon the first people. He let them out in groups, each speaking a different language.

FIJI

After Ndengei created humans, he showed them how to build canoes.

Allah sent rain from the heavens for people to drink, and olives and grapes for them to eat.

SAUDI ARABIA

The first humans slept in caves and lived like animals. The Sun Father felt sorry for them and sent two of his children to earth. "Watch what we do," they said, and they taught people how to till the soil and build houses, how to make shoes and how to weave wool.

PERU

GREECE

Two brother gods created animals and people. One gave animals strength and speed, wings and claws, and heavy fur for winter. "What's left for humans?" complained the other. To help them survive, he lit a torch from the sun and gave people fire.

MOZAMBIQUE

Once the first humans were made, the animals watched to see what they would do. They killed animals. They set fires in the forests, driving creatures from their homes. "They are burning and killing everything!" cried the god Mulungu.

GABON

God was angry with humankind. "Thunder, come!" he called. Thunder came running, Boom, boom, boom. "You and lightning shall set fire to the earth."

The gods met on a mountaintop and ordered the water god to flood the earth. Before he did, he went down and found one good couple. "Cut down an ahuehuete tree," he told them. "Ride it when the water comes."

MEXICO

God caused it to rain for forty days and forty nights. The water rose up the mountainsides, then higher than the peaks.

ISRAEL

CALIFORNIA

But Condor and his wife wove a
basket and floated in safety.

IRAQ

The great boat that Utnapishtim had built came to rest on a mountaintop. He released a dove. When it flew back, he knew the land was still under water. He freed a swallow. It came back as well. But when he released a raven, it never returned. It had found land.

NORWAY

The world was consumed with fire. But the World Tree that connects the earth with the heavens survived. Safe inside its bark were one man and one woman.

"Bring fire and an ear of corn," the water god had told the good couple. They'd done so. Slowly, the floodwaters receded until the couple could step onto land. The man dug a furrow. The woman planted a handful of corn kernels. The sun warmed the earth.